The History of
Glasney College

James Whetter

Tabb House
11 Church Street, Padstow, Cornwall

First published in Great Britain 1988
Tabb House, Church Street, Padstow, Cornwall, PL28 8BG.

*   *   *   *   *

Other historical works by the Author:

Cornwall in the Seventeenth Century
History of Falmouth

*   *   *   *   *

ISBN 0 907018 42 4

Typeset by St. George Printing Works Ltd, Commercial Centre,
Wilson Way, Pool Industrial Estate, Redruth, Cornwall, TR15 3QT.
Printed and bound by A. Wheaton and Co. Ltd.

Preface

THE establishment of the Friends of Glasney College Society at Penryn on 13th March, 1986, marks, we hope, a new stage in the study and investigation of this, probably the best known and most important of Cornwall's monastic institutions in the Middle Ages. In the last century much valuable work was done by G. Oliver, C. R. Sowell, and Thurstan Peter but a short succinct history of the college has never been available. It is hoped that this book fills the gap and will set the scene for deeper and more detailed investigations of aspects of its history. My main sources are indeed the published works of this trio and other historians (listed at the end) though my own researches on medieval Cornwall and the history of the Bodrugan family, which established a chantry at the college, have been useful, and have provided some additional bits of information.

I have avoided the use of footnotes and for further information on given topics readers should turn to the relevant sections in the published works.

James Whetter

*   *   *   *   *

rak Esyld

Contents

Tail pieces are taken from brasses in the churches mentioned in the captions.

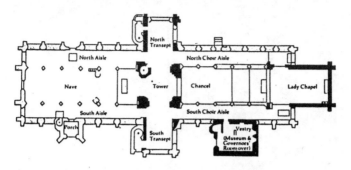

*Ground plan of Crediton Church, like Glasney modelled
on Exeter Cathedral. See p. 37.*

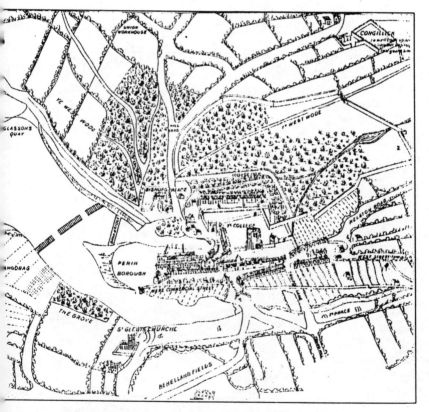

From Lord Burghley's map of Penryn and environs, c. 1580.

Glasney and Penryn from map c. 1540.

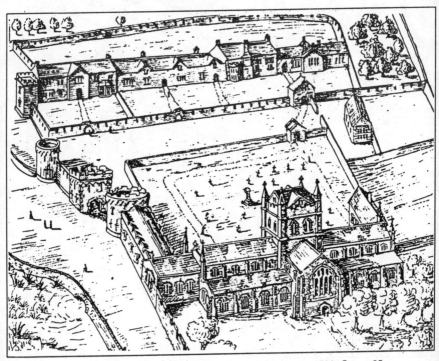

Sir Ferdinand George's reconstruction of Glasney c. 1580. See p. 35.

CHAPTER I

History

GLASNEY COLLEGE was unique among monastic institutions in Cornwall in that its foundation was not related to older and wider ranging movements or religious inspiration. Some of the smaller religious institutions date back to Celtic times and were composed of small groups of monks serving God in the way of early Christian tradition. Some of these institutions survived the Norman Conquest, such as St Buryan, Crantock, Probus, St Teath, Lamanna (St George's island, off Looe), but most were absorbed into larger institutions. St Anthony-in-Roseland became a cell of Augustinian canons and in 1140 became dependent on the priory of Plympton. St Cyret and Julette (St Carrok), north of Fowey, was seized by Robert, Count of Mortain around 1100 and became a cell of Cluniac monks, which his son later granted to the Priory of Montacute in Somerset. Following the English conquest of the tenth century, a Cornish bishopric was established at St Germans and a group of secular canons was set up in the cathedral. In 1180 they were established as a priory of Augustinian canons. At Launceston there was an early foundation of secular canons and this became a priory of Augustinian canons in 1127; later it was reputed to be the wealthiest priory in Cornwall. A Benedictine monastery was founded in Bodmin by Athelstan but this was subsequently destroyed by the Danes. The collegiate church which followed was taken over by Augustinian canons from Merton and this was established as a priory in 1124. Tywardreath was set up as a priory of Benedictine monks in 1088 and it became dependent on the abbey of St Serge in Normandy. An early Celtic monastery may have existed at St Michael's Mount though it is not certain whether there was a link between it and the pre-Norman conquest Benedictine priory established there by the eleventh century. About 1170 it was granted by Robert Count of Mortain to the Breton abbey of Mont St Michael and before achieving independent status was a cell of the Abbey. A Dominican friary was established at Truro in 1259 and the following year a Franciscan one at Bodmin.

Perhaps it was as a counter to the progress of the friars in Cornwall that in 1265 Bishop Walter Bronescombe of Exeter established Glasney College, strictly under his control and in an area where he had substantial interests. Similar colleges of canons were set up then or later at Crediton and Ottery St Mary in Devon by the Exeter bishops. The move to Glasney no doubt had economic and political overtones as it clearly had the support of the main power in Cornwall at this time, Richard, Earl of Cornwall, for several of his officials comprised the first officers of the college. In a similar way in 1114 Tavistock Abbey had been granted control over the cell at Tresco, on the Isles of Scilly, by King Henry I, in order to maintain supervision over the distant islands. The thirteenth century was a time of growing trade and population and the west of Cornwall and the Fal estuary were becoming areas of greater interest and economic activity. In 1236 Bishop Brewer secured the establishment of a weekly market for his town of Penryn and when completed, the college with its sea defence works and strong towers, as well as satisfying religious needs, was clearly designed to protect the town and its trading activity.

Overtly, the college was founded as a result of a dream Bishop Bronescombe had when he returned from a state visit to Germany on behalf of Richard the Earl. He was taken ill at Canterbury and in delirium three times in a vision saw Thomas Becket, who foretold his recovery, and told him on his return west, to found in the woods of Glasney in the episcopal manor of Penryn a collegiate church to the glory of God and in the name of St Thomas the Martyr:

This shall be to thee a sign. When thou comest to the place, Glasney, thou shalt search for a certain spot in it near the River of Antre, called by the inhabitants Polsethow, which Cornish name being interpreted is 'mire, or a pit' — which said place hath of old time borne such a name from the fact, that wild animals in the neighbourhood when wounded by an arrow, were wont to run thither after the nature and custom of such animals, and to plunge into its depth, and arrows could never be discovered there. And thou shalt find in it a large willow tree, and therein a swarm of bees; and there thou shalt appoint the High Altar and ordain the fabric. Of which said place it hath been anciently prophesied: 'In Polsethow shall habitations, or marvellous things be seen'.

On his recovery the bishop sped to Penryn and found the site much as described, marshy and overgrown. He located the willow tree and swarm of bees. Convinced of the truth of the vision, he spread abroad knowledge of it and with the aid of workmen cleared the site, rooted up the willow, channelled the river to the sea, and dried and levelled the area by means of earth brought down from higher parts.

To emphasise the holiness of the site, the writer continued in the cartulary of the college: 'In which said place of oft-times in the blackness of night a most brilliantly shining light was seen from Heaven and girt round with burning candles a multitude of clerks clad in white, praising God there; as is most positively testified by the neighbours, who told how they themselves saw these things'. The explanation for the lights might well be, more mundanely, emanations of marsh gas from the boggy land.

Work on the site was sufficiently far advanced for the bishop to lay the foundation on 'the morrow of the Annunciation of Our Lady' (Thursday, 25th March) 1265. Within two years the buildings, a church modelled on that of Exeter cathedral, refectory, and chapter house, with mills to the south in the area now known as Hill Head — were completed. On Sunday, the day after the festival of the Annunciation of Our Lady, 27th March, 1267, he consecrated the church and churchyard, the college having twin dedications to the visionary inspiration of the project, St Thomas Becket, and to the Virgin Mary, an increasingly popular cult figure in the Middle Ages.

For his house of secular canons the bishop devised a constitution modelled on that of the chapter of Exeter cathedral. He saw that it was appropriate to have as a bolster for his growing town of Penryn, in the centre of his west Cornwall estate, a college consisting of leading religious figures in the area: 'thirteen discreet persons of the more substantial sort in the same county'. Out of his own wood adjoining he provided each canon with one acre of ground to the south of the college on which to construct a house and other buildings for his occupation. Each was provided with an annual portion of £4 and to aid them in their work of religious celebration, thirteen priest-vicars were also appointed.

The names of the founding canons illustrate the influences that were at work in the establishment of the college and what purpose the strong-minded bishop wished them to serve. Several had close ties with the powerful earl of Cornwall. While the first head of the college, Henry de Bollegh, was the bishop's own clerk, three had connections with the earl or his administration: Sir Stephen Haym, also rector of Lanteglos and Lanivet, was his steward; Roger de Constantine, rector of Paul, Newlyn East and Lanreath, was his clerk; and Pagan de Lyskeryt, rector of St Stephen in Brannel, was his treasurer. Richard Vivian, rector of Lamorran, was the official who looked after the bishop's peculiars in Cornwall while other founding canons were established clergymen holding benefices in and round the Fal estuary: Nicholas de Tregorrek, rector of Constantine, Roland de Podyforth, rector of Creed, William de Saint Just, rector of St Just in Roseland, Robert Fitz-Robert, rector of Gwinear, Walter Peverell, rector of Ladock, Walter de Fermesham, rector of Mylor, Walter de Tremur, rector of Probus and Durandus Haym, probably a relative of the earl's steward, rector of Morwinstow. In many ways it was a sort of clerical club, though with political and economic overtones, of the notable and substantial clergymen of mid-Cornwall in the 1260s, an instrument of power and influence for both the bishop and the earl.

In a charter dated 26th March, 1267, the bishop initially endowed the college with the churches of Budock and Feock. In 1270 more churches were appropriated to the use of Glasney, 'considering the tenuity of the revenues of the church and the charge incumbent for the support of clerks ministering there'. The churches were Sithney, Zennor, St Goran, St Enoder, and

Kea, with the chapels of Kenwyn and Tregavethan, the bishop retaining the right to appoint the vicars. In this grant reference was made for the first time to the college having as its head a provost who was to 'have the care of it'.

Despite their collaboration over the founding of Glasney, the earl and bishop were soon to fall out. In December 1269 Roger de Valletort granted to Bishop Bronescombe and his successors the manor of Cargaul with the advowsons of the churches of St Newlyn and St Allen, an arrangement to which the earl took exception. Master Jordan, Archdeacon of Cornwall, and other ecclesiastics were assaulted at St Allen and in the park at Cargaul, their habits being torn and their horses ill-treated. The earl's steward, John Beaupre, subsequently acknowledged his part in the attacks, the damage done to the park and also the seizure and gaoling of Master John de Esse, chancellor of the diocese and official-principal. He promised to make pecuniary recompense as did other participants, though not all their names were known. In December 1274 Henry de Bollegh as provost of Glasney and the official of the Archdeacon of Cornwall were commissioned to search out and excommunicate the offenders and in March 1275 were instructed to deal with those who had dared to speak with those who had been excommunicated. However, in April Henry de Bollegh, the official, and a canon of Crediton were authorised to receive back 'into the bosom of the church' those who had been acting under the orders of others or who would give satisfaction for their offences. This followed a composition between the bishop and the earl regarding this and other disputes. Among other terms the earl undertook to remedy the damage done to the park of Cargaul, to recognise its liberties in future, and to re-erect the pillory and tumbrel of the borough of Penryn which had been thrown down.

However, more trouble ensued between the bishop and Earl Edmund (who had succeeded his father on his death in 1272) a few years later. When at Glasney in August 1277 Bishop Bronescombe addressed a letter to his four archdeacons concluding 'Wherefor you shall denounce as being fallen under the sentence of excommunication William de Tavistocke, Thomas Noel, Osbert Marck, Noel de Trevilla, Peter de

Marscalle, John de Sicca Villa and John le Portel, who after legal warning, had removed, and still were removing, some of the actual soil of the sanctuary of St Milor church, thereby diminishing the said sanctuary and doing wrong and injury to the right and liberty of the said church'. Presumably they were taking sand for use on the fields and this was probably an aspect of the dispute between the bishop and the earl concerning their respective rights to the foreshore. On 12th November, 1278, the bishop appointed proctors in the causes between himself and the earl and on the same day in his register there is a record that an agreement had been made between them by aid of mutual friends. The bishop agreed not to make exactions of the people of Cornwall in future against their will and released from excommunication those who had suffered in that way in the case. 'And as to the sands of St Milor, it was provided that three knights, men of experience, on behalf of the earl, and a like number on behalf of the bishop, should visit the place, and on their oaths lay down the limits between that which appertained to the church of St Milor, and that which was common to all; so that none should thenceforth take of the one without due payment made to the Parson, and the remainder should be common'. The bishop set his seal to this and as far as can be ascertained that was the end of the affair.

In 1275 the bishop established what became known as the de Ponte chantry and for its maintenance provided the benefice of Manaccan. In 1276 he assigned to Glasney the church of Colan for the purposes of celebrating the memory of St Gabriel the Archangel, who was his patron saint. Following the death of the founding bishop, his successor Peter Quivil put on a firmer footing the leadership of the college. While Henry de Bollegh and Walter de Fermesham certainly acted as heads of Glasney, the new bishop formalised the process and gave charge of the college in 1283 to a provost, who was to be a priest residing for at least two terms in the year and was to exercise the same jurisdiction over the canons and clerks as the dean had over the canons and clerks at Exeter cathedral. The first provost was William de Bodrugan, and at the same time the bishop assigned to the provostship the church of Probus. It soon appeared, however, that the latter arrangement was an error as Probus had already been given to the treasurer of the cathedral. In 1288 the matter was remedied and the church of Mylor appropriated to the use of the provost. In 1287 Bishop Quivil assigned a further benefice for the support of the college, the church of St Allen. In his donation he referred 'to the scandal that would fall on the church, if such an institution as Glasney was allowed to fall into decay and stating that the duties of the thirteen canons and the thirteen vicars in the night and day services in honour of God, the Blessed Virgin Mary and Thomas, archbishop and martyr, were very heavy, especially as some of the canons were frequently absent'.

William de Bodrugan was of an important Cornish landed family, which previously had been much involved with the priory of Tywardreath. William's father, Philip, had a good relationship with Bishop Bronescombe and when in 1259 the latter made a peregrination of Cornwall for the purpose of dedicating churches he stayed one night at the manor of Bodrugan. In 1269 Philip granted the bishop the advowson of St Goran, which was then appropriated to Glasney. As a second son, William went into the church and in 1274 became rector of the family benefice of St Martins-by-Looe. In July 1278 he succeeded to the canonry of Master William de Sancto Justo at Glasney and in April 1283 Quivil appointed him the first official provost of the college. William was involved in the dispute with the treasureship of Exeter over the advowson of Probus and, to establish the college's rights, he sent in his servants to levy distresses on the lands of one Martin, son of Reginald de St Probus. This dispute was resolved in 1288 in favour of the treasureship but William Bodrugan had more success earlier, in 1284, when before the itinerant justices he and his chapter won a contest over the advowson of Kenwyn church. In return for his concessions they promised to pray for their opponent, John de Ryvers, for eternity in the customary offices at their church of St Thomas the Martyr.

King Edward I vowed to go on a crusade and in 1288 Pope Nicholas IV sanctioned the raising of a tenth for six years towards defraying its cost. However, popular feeling was running another way and Edward I launched a campaign against the Jews in

England which had more support. But the clergy backed the king in his original mission and voted a tenth of their income to him, for which Edward had a new valuation roll prepared that was completed in 1291. The resulting 'Taxation of Pope Nicholas IV' is of much value to scholars in showing the relative wealth of the church at this time; elsewhere the available details are given that relate to the benefices held by Glasney. It provoked much bitter controversy at the time and complaints were numerous that the valuations were frequently much too high. Undoubtedly it was a factor in the struggle between the clergy and the king later in the decade.

William de Bodrugan relinquished the position of provost in February 1288 but he was still a rising star and in 1295 became Archdeacon of Cornwall. It was during his tenure of this important office that the crisis between Edward I and the clergy came to a head. In 1296 Pope Boniface VIII issued a bull, *Clericis Laicos*, forbidding the clergy from granting aid to secular authorities out of ecclesiastical sources. A bitter dispute followed and in 1297, certain recalcitrant clergy were imprisoned for refusing to support the king. In Cornwall thirty of their number were sent to Launceston gaol, while William de Bodrugan was fined for publishing the bull. It is not known whether priests from Glasney were involved though it would seem likely in view of William's association with the place and the important position it had by this time achieved in West Cornwall. The king made some concessions but it was eventually the clergy who had to give way. In February, 1298, goods and chattels seized from the archdeacon were returned and the ecclesiastical prisoners released. On William's death in 1308 he was remembered with respect at Glasney and as canon and priest his obit was thereafter held each year on the day of his death, 9th August.

His nephew, Henry de Bodrugan, also had a connection with the college, albeit of a different character. Henry was in dispute with Thomas Lercedekne and Ralph Bloyou, members of two old and established families, over the wardship of an heir Hugh de Treverbyn. Henry withdrew with his ward to a house of a canon at Glasney, William Bloyou. At a subsequent inquisition the jury stated that a certain Ralph Bloyou together with others unknown, came to the house of the said Thomas Lercedekne on the said Friday at Landegy (Churchtown Farm, Old Kea) and the same Ralph and Thomas together with a certain Thomas de Tremur and Henry de Sulgheny, servants of the same Thomas, having had conference there, armed themselves with padded tunics and military tunics and other arms, taking with them swords, knives, lances, etc., and thence rode armed with the others to the house of one William Bloyou at Glasney, where Henry de Bodrugan was then staying. And in the night by force and arms wounded and maltreated him and seized the said heir from his custody, and abducted the heir to the house of Thomas Lercedekne at Landegy. . .

Lercedekne and Ralph Bloyou later were imprisoned at Launceston and Henry de Bodrugan was given 100 marks as compensation. The Bodrugan-Bloyou feud continued, however, and it was not to end until Ralph was committed to gaol again, where he died. It is not known where Henry was buried on his death in 1307; probably at St Goran in which parish the home manor of Bodrugan lay; but showing the attachment of the family for the place, on the death of his widow, Sybil, she was buried within the church at Glasney.

The fourteenth century probably saw Glasney at the height of its influence and popularity. The college reached the full scope of its holdings, new chantries were added and, especially in the later part of the century, new work was carried out on the buildings. In the middle years the place had the enthusiastic backing and support of a Bishop of Exeter, John Grandisson (1326-69), so much so that he was described as a second founder of the college. Gifts were made by devout persons in order that they would be remembered in the church's ministrations. In November 1315 Master William de Mulleborne, rector of Ruan Lanihorne, left a quarter of an acre of land adjoining St Thomas's Street, in order that prayers be said for the souls of Bishop Walter Stapeldon and himself, 8s. being paid out of the said land as was customary to lay on divine service and to provide for the distribution of bread to the poor. In January 1321 Benedict Arundel, one of the canons, quit claimed to the church land at Polventon, probably in St Gluvias parish, so that the college could expend 6s. 8d. on the anniversary of the donor, 11th July, for a mass, after payments to the canons, vicars, and other ministers present, the residue being given to the poor in bread. In November 1336 for a similar purpose Stephen de Hal of Penryn and his wife, Marguria, granted 3s. in silver to be paid on 1st March of every year, secured on a messuage in the borough. For obits for themselves, William, son of Roger de Bodwey granted in 1349 a pension of 8s. yearly payable on 26th October, secured on a messuage; John Rouse of Penryn and Constance his wife granted a similar sum in 1356; and on her husband's death in 1377, Constance gave 4s. annual rent from a tenement by the church of St Mary, Penryn for a yearly obit to be celebrated for her soul on the feast of All Saints. Odo Brasigonha granted 8s. yearly rent out of a messuage in Penryn for an obit for himself on 14th June, 1369 and on 9th July, 1380 Walter Myn, vicar of St Gluvias, and John Trevyda granted the chapter of Glasney a similar sum for the same purpose out of three messuages in Penryn.

The most important officer at the college after the provost was the sacristan, the first recorded one being Robert de Trethelw; this from the Kalendar of Obits in the surviving Glasney Cartulary. Among his duties were the care of vessels and vestments, the superintendence of the cleaning of the church and the opening and closing of the gates and doors. In 1315 to enable him to carry out his work the better, the church of St Colan was appropriated for his use. It is clear that it was following this decision of Bishop Stapeldon that the first fully-fledged sacristan was established at Glasney and Robert Trethelw, alias Sir Robert de Tredowel, was appointed to the position. As well as being vicar of St Gluvias, he also held the post of warden of the college, though normally the holding of more than one office was against the rules. It was not a popular position as responsibilities were heavy and rewards few. It was probably to make it more secure that in 1334 Bishop Grandisson appointed Robert de Tredowel, still the sacristan, to the prebend then vacated by Otho de Northwode. Thereafter the same prebend was annexed to the office.

The close ties established with the Bodrugan family went a stage further in 1329 with the establishment of a Bodrugan chantry, for which purpose Otto de Bodrugan granted Bishop Grandisson the advowson of Mevagissey church. Otto was a leading figure in Cornwall at this time and appears to have been conscientiously religious, having at Bodrugan his own chapel and chaplain. Two of his six sons, John and Thomas, went into the church, the former holding a prebend at Glasney from 1342 to 1349. He himself went on a pilgrimage to St James of Compostella in 1324. In 1331 he began a longer journey to the Holy Land. He reached Bordeaux, but travelling overland to the Mediterranean coast he must have become ill, for he died at Montpellier on 6th September, being buried at a monastery there, either the Benedictine monastery of St Maurice de Sauret or the Cluniac priory of St Peter de Clunesel. At Glasney his obit was celebrated, in the same manner as for a canon, thereafter on the anniversary of his death.

Life at the college appears to have pursued a fairly normal course in the 1330s and 1340s. While danger signs of poverty and pressure of population hung over the land, the college, having ironed out early organisational difficulties, had settled into a regular pattern of existence and had become a respected and appreciated partner for the adjacent town and port of Penryn, itself growing in trade and prosperity. Canons of the college, frequently leading churchmen in the area, were called upon to undertake tasks of importance. The 1340s were preoccupied with the wars in France, culminating in the English triumph at Crecy in 1347. The wars put in a new light monastic houses which were dependent on alien churches — such as Tywardreath Priory and St Michael's Mount — and those, like Glasney, not linked in this way must have benefited in terms of popular appreciation and support.

In 1349 Cornwall, like the rest of Britain, was swept by the great climacteric of the Middle Ages, the Black Death; an event which changed the whole course and outlook of medieval society. It is generally estimated that more than a third of the population died, the clergy being as much affected as lay members of the population. The number of institutions of priests to Cornish benefices averaged annually 4.2 before 1349. In the twelve months commencing March 1349 no less than eighty-five institutions were made, more than twenty times the usual number. At Bodmin priory, the prior John de Kilkhampton died in February and shortly after all the canons save two. In March these two survivors wrote in pathetic terms to the bishop saying that they were 'like orphans' and entreating him to appoint a superior for their house as soon as possible. Other casualties at around this time were the master of St John's hospital, Helston, the dean of Crantock, and the priors of Minster and St Michael's Mount. Glasney was not immune. Five vacancies were filled in 1349: William de Tregoney was collated as sacristan on 24th April, on the 3rd May John de Oldestowe succeeded to the prebend of Thomas de Crouthorne of Crediton, on 8th June Stephen Pempel succeeded to that of Henry Broke, on 10th September William de Carslake to that of Master de Stokes, and the same month Master Otho de Northwode to that of John de Bodrugan, all whom they replaced presumably having succumbed to the plague.

In spite of all that, the college and the community of which it formed part survived, revived. Bishop Grandisson still held sway at Exeter and in 1355 was pleased to promote a further addition to the college. Sir John de Beaupre or Bello Prato gave the bishop the advowson of St Just in Penwith after finding that 'the vicars of Glasney were not receiving enough of their accustomed stipends to afford them a sufficient livelihood, owing to the recent pestilence, the change in the times, and the growing malice of men, and therefore desired to increase their stipends and to augment their number'. After the death of the rector of St Just, the college was to enter into possession of the rectory, appointing a vicar to serve there while two additional priests, nominated by Sir John, were to join the college.

To get across the Christian message to the largely illiterate populace pictorial means were employed in medieval churches. Wall paintings, carvings, and ornamental glass were all used to depict religious scenes and to recreate holy events. As early as the thirteenth century dramatic re-enactments of biblical and other episodes were being performed in churches to enlighten and impress the multitude. It was out of these that the Cornish Miracle plays grew, the Passion and Resurrection plays and others about Cornish saints. The naves of churches were commonly used for the staging of such dramas, while trade guilds often took up their production. Complaints developed that the message of the plays were being lost, with combats being staged, secular intrusions and ribaldry. In 1360 there was a record of the acting of plays during the Christmas holidays and on certain Saints' days in several religious establishments in the diocese. On 10th December Bishop Grandisson issued a prohibition addressed to churches at Ottery and Crediton, Exeter cathedral and to the provost and chapter of Glasney forbidding, under pain of excommunication, such unseemly and improper pastimes. Each of them in reply gave an undertaking to put a stop to the abuse and, as he had also ordered, to transcribe the bishop's mandate in their missals and in other service books.

Additional work was being carried out on the church in the late 1360s and by his will of 8th September, among other things, Bishop Grandisson bequeathed twenty marks to Glasney for new work there. In 1379 William Carslake, one of the canons, left £20 to the new work on the church. The death of the bishop caused some problems in the college because as was common practice during episcopal vacancies the king claimed the right of nomination to benefices and other ecclesiastical positions that came vacant in the diocese. Robert Hoo was collated provost by Grandisson's successor, Thomas Brantyngham, but in a writ of 29th November, 1370, addressed to the sheriff, the king ordered the lands of the bishop and Robert Hoo to be seized and for them to appear before him to show cause why he should not present to the vacant provostship. In January 1371 the justices decided the matter in the king's favour and he nominated Sir Reginald Calle whom shortly afterwards the bishop commissioned his official-peculiar in Cornwall to admit. But the dispute was not yet over; the papal nuncio claimed rights of 'first-fruits' in respect of Hoo's provision but this was resisted by the crown. The nuncio eventually relaxed the sequestration and cancelled the censures. Hoo, however, hoping the death of Calle might give him the provostship and in the words of Thurstan Peter 'unwilling to await the course of nature' attacked him in the precincts of Glasney church and nearly killed him. He and his accomplice fled and went into hiding for three years. On 10th January, 1375, the bishop excommunicated him and on 3rd March deprived him of any right he may have had under the papal provision. Calle, (whether as a result of the assault is not known), appears to have declined in health and in September 1373 had the right to celebrate in his own house in the church close. On 3rd February, the following year, he wrote to the bishop requesting a co-adjutor: 'Like the Elder Toby, I sit in darkness and cannot see the light of heaven'. On the 15th the bishop granted his request.

Certainly, during the late fourteenth century an unsettled atmosphere appears to have developed. On 29th March, 1379 the bishop addressed a commission to the official-peculiar in Cornwall and Sir Geoffrey Carew, sacristan of Glasney (the provost being ill), to inquire into and correct 'the crimes, excesses, and negligences of the canons, ministers, and servants of the college and in cases of contumacy to appoint others in their place. Some of the unrest clearly related to the Wycliffite movement and the peasants' revolt of 1381. The following year Bishop Brantyngham issued a mandate to the main religious leaders of Cornwall, including provost Walter Myn, against 'Laurence Bedeman who goeth around in vestments, and having entered our fold secretly with fraud, and stealthily under the feigned image of holiness, with foxlike crafts, endeavours in his public and private discourses, to turn aside our sheep and to lead them into the various errors of heresy: therefore being desirous to chase away such a fox from our fold lest he worry our sheep' the bishop ordered inquiries to be made and for Bedeman to appear before him. As it turned out Bedeman does not seem to have been such a bad lad. On examination by the bishop later in the year he proved himself to be a true catholic and no heretic and in 1383 was instituted rector of the Devon parish of Lifton.

Dissatisfaction was expressed with Walter Myn's successor as provost, John Edneves. In a commission addressed to the official-peculiar and archdeacon of Cornwall and others in March 1384 the bishop ordered an investigation into reports respecting his activities. He was alleged to have uttered 'vile enormities against the authority and dignity of Pope Urban VI, King Richard, and the bishops of England, and especially his own bishop, which things he asserted, talked about, and publicly preached in the college and in other places, rejecting the bishop's jurisdiction and bringing it into open contempt'. As it chanced, it was found the troublesome provost had infringed the canon against pluralities by already holding the perpetual vicarage of the parish church of Sutton in Plymouth and the bishop was able to secure his ejection.

It was during the provostship of his successor, Sir John Raufe, that violence occurred in the church yard of Glasney. Sir John Poghlande, priest and a vicar at Glasney, had come to blows with Robert, a tithing man of Treliever. Little is known of the incident except that a commission of 16th September, 1386 was directed to Master William Hendre, official-peculiar in Cornwall to investigate the matter, 'the cemetery of Glasney having been polluted by violence'. Clearly the atmosphere at the college had deteriorated and in the following year, in a commission of 26th January addressed to Richard Colshull, canon at the college, Bishop Brantyngham said that after his recent visitation he had tried without success to amend the grave excesses and offences of the canons and other ministers that he had discovered, but had been informed that they were still leading dissolute lives, even harbouring women of doubtful character in their houses. The commissioners were to investigate and report back. Later in the same year, the bishop made another official visit and found that 500 marks belonging to the college treasury, as well as ornaments and vestments which had been given or bequeathed to the church had been dispersed and were in the hands of persons unknown. Subsequently a commission was directed to a later provost, William Cullyng, to make investigations.

Problems continued, however, and in June 1395 John Rowe, canon and steward, was excommunicated for attempting to defraud William Cullyng of the fruits and privileges of his prebend. On his accession to the bishopric, Edmund Stafford made a determined effort to remedy the situation. Following a visitation in September 1400 and finding many things in need of correction he issued a long list of orders to improve the running of the college. All vicars and inferior ministers guilty of neglect and irreverence in saying the divine offices should be punished by the provost or sacristan, in his absence, in open chapter, not in their chambers or privately. No canon should hinder a vicar from doing his proper duty by imposing upon him any domestic service and vicars should not be allowed leave of absence too freely — too many of them on the same side of the choir should not have leave at the same time. Canons should be present in their proper habit at the divine offices and at mass, as the statutes required, and vicars should say their masses at such times as not to interfere with the recitation of the hours in the choir, which they themselves were bound to attend. None of them, whether in their habits or not, should presume to walk about the church or its precincts in service time. Canons in residence should regularly, in succession, week by week, say high mass at the high altar unless they had a reasonable excuse when provision should be made for a replacement. The common seal was to be kept securely under three keys, one in charge of the provost or his locum tenens, the others with two of the canons and it was never to be used except with the consent of the majority of the senior canons. The sacristan or his clerk should attend carefully to ringing the bells for the services, closing the screens, gates, and doors of the church and the gate of the close, in good time, lest damage happen to the church or scandal to the ministers and should provide bread and wine, pure and not acid, daily for mass and cleanse the vessels used at the altar. If negligent, on the third occasion, he should be dismissed with a month's notice by the sacristan.

The provost and his chapter promised obedience to these orders and also gave support to the scheme for repairs and new building work. On his visitation the bishop found that the church was in need of repair and that part was incomplete, in particular the arches and vaulting of the choir and the choir-aisles. 'All were anxious to help forward the work' and agreed to devote the whole of their stipends for one year to aid the work, except the sacristan Geoffrey Carew, and John Raff, a canon, who alone held no benefices outside the college; even they, however, agreed to reduced stipends, £20 and 10 marks for the year respectively. The bishop sanctioned the proposals and put in charge as receivers Alan Treles, rector of the de Ponte chantry, and Thomas Trefuthon, one of the vicars-choral, who were to lay out the money with the advice of the Archdeacon of Cornwall, Edward Dauntesey, and Canon Matthew Bodrigy.

The relationship of the archdeacon to the college had not always been a happy one. In 1331 Bishop Grandisson had complained that the officers of the archdeacon had intruded into the deanery of Penryn, which included the college, though it was well known this was a bishop's peculiar and exempt from archidiaconal jurisdiction. Part of the trouble appears to have been that one of the prebends had been annexed to the archdeacon's office in the time of Bishop Bronescombe and this had given him a foothold in the place. On this occasion Bishop Grandisson appears to have taken away the prebend 'for contumacy'. However, in 1397 reconciliation seems to have been effected and Bishop Stafford annexed a prebend at the college permanently to the office of archdeacon.

Bishop Brantyngham, in addition to other actions (he remembered the church in his will of 13th December, 1393, granting it his 'red vestment with the copes and other parts of the suit') appears to have endowed a chantry at the college, for in 1396 there was a dispute which reached the court of Westminster over the advowson of the three chantries at Glasney: Brantyngham, Bodrugan, and Beaupre. By that year the rights of presentation to the three had been amalgamated and were then in the possession of William Hankford and with them the manor of Calenick and rents from Lanistley. It could be that the amalgamation was part of the alienation and removal of rights and goods that the bishops were complaining of at this time.

New blood in the Bodrugan family through the marriage of the chief justice, Sir Robert Hull, to the Bodrugan heiress, Joan, around 1405, as well as leading to the renovation and rebuilding of the manor's home farm at Gorran stimulated new interest in the Bodrugan chantry at Glasney. Co-operating in June 1407 with her son William (by a former marriage and who had adopted the Bodrugan name) they granted land at Treswithian to Thomas Lessynwor, the chaplain of the chantry at 'the altar called Bodrigannesauter', in order that thenceforward he should pray for the soul of the founder and those of Robert, Joan, and William after their deaths. From the proceeds of the land he was to have his maintenance and expenses for the management of the chantry.

The great infirmity of a vicar-choral, Thomas Chamberleyn, in August 1403, which prevented his getting about, was the cause of his being granted a licence to celebrate in any suitable place within the college enclosure. Some misdemeanours clearly occurred in the church in the early part of 1405 for in March a licence was granted to the provost and canons to celebrate in the common hall of the vicars until Pentecost, unless the church in the meantime had been reconciled. On the 29th of the same month the canons were licensed to celebrate in their residences within the close, and the others in the common hall, but that is the last that is heard of the matter and presumably not long after normal services were resumed. This was the great age of indulgences when remissions were granted for sins committed in return for contributions from the laity. In August 1410 an indulgence was granted to the faithful who should contribute to the maintenance and enrichment of the high altar in the church and visit the same on certain great festivals. The same year a commission was issued touching the delapidations caused by the neglect of a late canon, Walter Estcolm.

Glasney, like other religious establishments at this time, was slow in settling papal dues, first-fruits, Peter's pence, and the like. The reputation of the papacy with its rival popes was then at a low ebb. Between 1408 and 1410 the college was said to be three years in arrear of 'procurations' due to the pope's collector. There was little improvement in subsequent years and in 1421 the college was still three years behind in their payments. In 1423 like the officials of many other south-western institutions the provost was cited to appear before the papal collector in London and again in 1441.

The sacristan's duties were a matter of some dispute and as early as 1336 Bishop Grandisson had stressed that though continuous residence was enjoined on him it would suffice if he resided in the college for three of the four terms of the year. Master Nicholas Harry, who held the office in 1424, appears to have been something of an awkward customer. Bishop Edmund Lacy, writing that year to the Dean of Kerrier and Sir John

Rawlyn, vicar-choral of Glasney, insisted that Master Harry obey the judgement of the commissaries in a dispute between himself and his chapter, whereby he was bound to undertake the repair of the books and ornaments of the church. The sacristan stood firm, however, and among other things claimed that no minister could leave the college without his leave, that at greater-double feasts he should lead in divine service and that in the absence of the provost he should be president of the canons sitting in chapter. When the provost was present he claimed second place. The whole business was put to the arbitration of William Fylham, Canon of Exeter and Archdeacon of Cornwall, and Richard Oliver, Canon of Glasney and Rector of Allington in Devon. On 18th November, 1427 they reported their decision that no one could leave the college without the permission of the sacristan, and that in the absence of the provost the senior canon and not the sacristan was to take precedence. They added, however, that as to the repair of books, vestments and ornaments their previous decision still stood.

Master Walter Trengofe, collated provost in September 1427, had had a distinguished ecclesiastical career; educated at Exeter College, Oxford, he had become rector there and later Chancellor of the University. He was illegitimate, a not unusual condition of clerics in the Middle Ages. Believed to be the son of the vicar of St Neot, John Trengofe, he had had dispensation to take orders in 1411. It was during his provostship in September 1435 that he and the chapter made a series of regulations regarding the college accounts. They provided that all moneys were to be kept in the same chest as the college seal, that two of the keys of that chest were to be kept by two custodians, and that no canon should be a custodian if notably indebted to the college. Clearly there was some suspicion of fiddling.

There were problems at the college in subsequent years. In July 1439 the official of the bishop's peculiar jurisdiction in Cornwall was ordered to enquire into alleged pollution by bloodshed of the churchyard at Glasney. It later appeared that blood had been spilt in a conflict there between one Peter Gerveys and another, unnamed, though no additional details are available. Following the visitation of the bishop in April 1445 he found much that was unsatisfactory. Because of the long lapse in work on the church, the buildings were still incomplete and the church largely in ruins. The levy of 26s. per annum on each of the eleven prebends to aid work on the fabric of the church was to be revived. Choristers had no suitable habitations and had been forced 'to roam around the town night and day'. In future they were to be restored to the chamber in which they used to live with the succentor. Mismanagement of the college's finances and property was also observed. Canons who had been stewards in former years and who had not rendered proper accounts were to do so by 24th June next and they were to restore to the common chest, kept locked with two locks, in the exchequer, all chapter properties which they had carried off to their lodgings, and in future all moneys were to be paid in and all disbursements made in the exchequer and not in private houses. The injunctions were to be enforced under threat of excommunication and those who disregarded them were to answer to the bishop himself.

In 1449 more problems surfaced and in July and September the bishop issued orders for an investigation to be made. Master Henry Webber, canon and treasurer of Exeter Cathedral, Sir Thomas Flygh also canon there, John Rawe, canon at Glasney, were instructed to 'correct, punish and reform abuses in the said collegiate church, if upon enquiry they find widespread reports of quarrels etc. to be true'. In 1451 the provost and canons had trouble with a neighbour, Henry Hogge, formerly of St Budock but then of St Gluvias. He was summonsed by the provost in a matter of perjury and breach of faith, but not responding, was excommunicated by the president of the Exeter consistory for 'his aggravated contumacy'.

But as today, it is always the bad news that gets the headlines, and in general life continued at the college in a fairly normal fashion, with services being regularly held, obits being said, and the residents ministering to local needs as an important and invigorating body in the local community. Though dates when they began are not available, some of the obits recorded in the college's kalendar were clearly initiated in the fifteenth century, in particular those of Joan, widow of Otto Killigrew, Otto Trevarthian who died around 1420, and Thomas Gwynow 'who gave £10 to the provost and chapter to celebrate the obits of himself and of one Ralph, for twenty years after their death, and to distribute yearly on the day of the said obit amongst the canons and other ministers of the church present at the exequies and mass, according to their degree'.

Moreover, the college was remembered in the wills of several prominent individuals in the fifteenth century. Hugh de Hyckelyng, a precentor of Exeter who had formerly been a canon of Glasney, left 40s. to the fabric of the church by his will of 8th August, 1415, while in 1430 Martin Lercedeene, a canon at Exeter, among other gifts to Cornish churches left his concordance (selected texts from the bible) to the college. James Michell, a canon of Glasney, left by his will of 21st October, 1438, one pound of wax to the light of St Thomas in the church and desired to be buried before the image of St Michael and the Archangel. By his will of 6th April, 1476, Thomas Enys among other bequests gave two pence to St Thomas the Martyr of Glasney.

Michael Trewinnard, a native of St Ives and Fellow of Exeter College, Oxford was provost, according to William Worcester, in the 1460s and died, the same authority said, on Maundy Thursday 1471 (11th April). His vicar was called Aunger and was the last contact, albeit a not auspicious one, between the college and the Bodrugan family; Henry Bodrugan, their last representative, was to lose all his lands in 1487 when attainted of treason by the Lancastrian regime. In a complicated case of 1473 the King's Constable of Devon, John Tanner, brought an action against the borough officials of Tregoney. He claimed that a Welsh priest had abducted a man's wife and John Aunger of Glasney had managed to release the woman and put her in safe keeping. However, the priest had got in touch with one Piers Mason and others, the servants of Henry Bodrugan, 'the then power in Cornwall'. Aunger, 'for fear of death', sought the support of John Tanner but Piers Mason and Bodrugan's men located him there and took him away. Meanwhile, Mason alleged that he had lost money and a ring at Tanner's house and was prosecuting him in the court of the portreeve of Tregoney. This reveals a sordid underworld that clearly Glasney College men occasionally participated in.

William Worcester, in his tour of Cornwall in 1478, gave some slight glimpses of life at the college. From Truro borough to Penryn it was six miles and from Penryn to Helston borough eight miles. 'Thursday, 17th September, St Lambert's day I heard mass at St Michael's Mount and the same afternoon I rode back to the town of Penryn. Friday 18th September I spent the night at Penryn where there is a College, and reached Bodmin'. After giving details of Michael Trewinnard, Worcester went on

The site of the said College in Penryn was anciently called 'Glasneyth' in the Cornish tongue, or in English 'Polsethow', otherwise Archer's Pool. . .Memorandum that Sir John Anger was vicar of Master Michael Trewinnard. . .1265. The church of the college, where Master Michael was chief provost of the canons and vicars, was founded there by Walter le Goode, Bishop of Exeter. And the bishop named Graundson was the second founder after the said Walter in his benefits to this church. The length of the said church, viz. its nave, is about fifty steps, and the length of the transepts, is by estimation only fifty steps. The length of the choir of the church with its ambulatory is about another fifty steps by estimation.

While Thurstan Peter and C. R. Sowell have disputed the value of these measurements (Worcester's step was of two foot length, it has been suggested) this is our first bit of hard evidence and description, brief though it is, of the college when it existed. Elsewhere it should be noted, however, Worcester gave a length of sixty steps both for the nave and the choir.

Apart from the brief involvement of John Aunger with Henry Bodrugan, members of the college appear to have steered clear of the rivalries involved in the Yorkist-Lancastrian conflict and such episodes as the siege of St Michael's Mount in 1473. During the provostship of Master John Pascow in 1489 the college played host to members of a royal expedition to Spain. To strengthen his dynasty Henry VII planned a treaty of alliance with the Spanish royal house, cemented by a marriage of his son Arthur with Katherine of Aragon. His Cornish supporter Sir Richard Nanfan was appointed ambassador, and accompanied by Dr Savage, the ambassador of Castile and his chaplain, the Richmond knight-at-arms, and the Herald of Scotland the party left Southampton on

19th, January 1489. However, their boat was forced into Plymouth and they stayed there until 1st February. Again by 'a great tempest of wind, rain and bad weather' they were forced to make harbour and came into Falmouth haven. Sir Richard Nanfan stayed with the provost and others with leading figures at Penryn, the ambassador with a merchant, John Luck, the knight, chaplain, and herald with Thomas Killigrew, and Dr Savage with Piers Luck. The party remained ten days, which must have occasioned much excitement in the area and put some strain on its resources to entertain them suitably.

On the retirement of Master Pascow in 1491, Sir John Oby succeeded as provost, being collated on 4th December. He had been instituted to a prebend initially in 1478, then described as a chaplain, and in 1479 had become sacristan. In 1492, like other Cornish religious houses, the college was subjected to a visitation by a commissary of Archbishop Morton, Robert Sherborne, treasurer of Hereford cathedral. Various deficiencies were noted by the residents. Master John Obey, the provost, said that they did not say matins '*in media nocte*' according to the statutes and did not have dispensation. Master William Nicholl, the sacristan, pointed out that they should have had thirteen vicars but only had seven; the provost was ordered to make up the number. He also said that the late provost, Master John Pascow, had erased the statutes as to divers things relating to the office of provost, so that no one knew what should be done by the provost in connection with divine service. It appeared that three of the houses of non-residents were not well repaired, 'for they are almost entirely destroyed' and the commissary accordingly took in hand the profits of the prebends. Master William Peres said that they were bound by the statutes to distribute annually 40s. to the poor but they did not pay a penny. All were agreed, though, that they did not have sufficient funds for this. Of the vicars, Sir John Aunger complained that the vicars' steward did not pay them what he had received for that purpose and made the point that the statutes were not publicly read. The last was also mentioned by other residents and the college was given until Michaelmas to equip themselves with written statutes. A fairly thorough investigation revealed that the college had been going through a bad period.

But it was nothing to what was to afflict the provost in the summer of 1497. Sir John Oby had clearly become quite an important figure in the west of Cornwall and had a good relationship with the secular authorities. In January parliament had voted a heavy tax for the king's Scottish wars, two whole fifteenths and tenths payable in May and November, and a further subsidy of £120,000. Sir John was appointed a collector in the west of Cornwall and his scrupulosity in administering the taxes, which hit all sections of the population, began to cause resentment. While the people valued the church for various aspects of its ministrations there were features that were never popular; the obligation to pay a tenth of the produce of crops and livestock, (that on corn and hay being called the great tithes or garb,) that on lesser items, the small tithes, being the main one. Sometimes the tithes of parishes were leased or 'farmed' and this was a cause of upset when the 'farmers' were seen to be profiting from the system. In these circumstances if churchmen appeared to be living too well and not paying enough attention to their duties anger could grow. The head of the church in England, Archbishop Morton, a close adviser of the king, was held partly responsible for the levying of the taxation in 1497. As his visitation had shown in 1492, there was some laxity in the college's affairs and since the place had control of much of the tithe collection in the area, it no doubt had begun to attract resentment. It is probably significant that several from the neighbourhood of Penryn played an active part in the rebellion of that summer.

St Keverne people began to stir under the leadership of a blacksmith, Michael Joseph. Others joined in and they marched to Bodmin where local gentry, the lawyer Thomas Flamank, and others reinforced their numbers. Gathering recruits as they went, the rebels marched into Devon and on to Wells where James Lord Audley gave them support. The rest of the story is well-known; the march to Blackheath, the eventual and inevitable defeat, the execution of Michael Joseph and Thomas Flamank at Tyburn on 27th June, and the beheading of Audley the same day at the Tower. However, the Cornish were 'little mollified or quieted' and on the arrival of the Yorkist pretender to the throne, Perkin

Warbeck, at Whitsand bay on 7th September he quickly gained a following; it is clear pro-Yorkist feelings were a factor in both risings. He left his wife in the custody of the priests of St Michael's Mount and marched rapidly to Bodmin where he proclaimed himself Richard IV. His rebellion attracted some 3,000 supporters in Cornwall but was soon to fizzle out after an abortive attempt to take Exeter. With reduced numbers he marched to Taunton but his courage failed with the approach of the royal army under Daubeney and on 21st September he slipped away from the main force. It was at this unfortunate stage that Sir John Oby was met by a band of sea-rovers who had come to aid Perkin Warbeck under the lead of one James. What he was doing in the area is not known; perhaps attending the Bishop of Exeter, perhaps trying to get out of harm's way from the Cornish rebels. However, his exactions were remembered. It was said that he had 'gathered more money than came into the King's use'. He was taken to Taunton and 'there in the market-place (they). . . slew him piteously, in such wise that he was dismembered and cut in many and sundry pieces' — the most frightening end of any of the Glasney provosts.

His fate, though, should not be too closely related to that of the college. Only three years later, Thomas Killigrew, a leading figure in the locality, both landed proprietor and merchant, bequeathed the substantial sum of 100 marks (£66.13s.4d.) for restoring the church. In 1510 John Enys made bequests to local churches, including 12d. to the image of St Thomas the Martyr in Glasney. Its role as a social and ecclesiastical centre continued; indeed, an even more significant role emerged in this period which was to be of lasting value for the revival of Cornish cultural individuality, its language in modern times.

Sir John Oby was succeeded as provost by Master John Nans, collated on 29th November, 1497 by Bishop Redmayne at Torre. On 5th June, 1501 a double ceremony took place at Exeter by which John Nans exchanged the provostship and the vicarage of St Gluvias for the benefices of Camborne and Illogan, while their former holder, Master Alexander Penhylle, took on the provostship and St Gluvias. It is in this period that it is believed religious or miracle plays were composed at the college in the

Cornish language. That Cornish was the vernacular tongue of Penryn and the area is shown by the rather superior comments of the Venetian ambassador when delayed at the haven in 1506: 'We are in a very wild place which no human being ever visits, in the midst of a most barbarous race, so different in language and custom from the Londoners and the rest of England that they are as unintelligible to these last as to the Venetians'. Outside of the church services it is clear it was Cornish that was spoken in the cloisters of Glasney, no doubt until the end of its days, and obviously before. And when dramas were performed on feast days to brighten and enlighten the lives of the local population it was in Cornish that their lively stories unfolded.

The early months of 1506 when Master Alexander Penhylle was still provost saw the detention through bad weather of a royal party at Falmouth, King Philip of Spain and Queen Juana as well as the Venetian ambassador to Castile. As the only major institution by the lower reaches of the estuary, it is likely the college played host to the celebrated visitors. Maybe it was a rather boisterous and rowdy production of a Cornish miracle play in Glasney church that so bemused and amazed the cultivated gentleman from Venice. On the resignation of Master Penhylle in 1507 he was succeeded by another Cornishman, Master William Uryn, collated on 24th March. In 1509 the accession of Henry VIII, independent and wilful, betokened a new and uncomfortable era. Among other things, the monarch subsequently took exception to the memory of St Thomas Becket and it was felt advisable to emphasise the other dedication of the college to the Blessed Virgin Mary.

The king's conflict with the papacy deepened in the 1520s and '30s and on 17th August, 1534 the then provost, James Gentle, subscribed to the king's supremacy, along with John Chymmowe, sacristan, James Treveth, John Knebone and Ralph Trelabys, canons. Another subscriber was Warin Penhalluryk, vicar of Wendron, who was also a prebendary of Glasney. Later in the year parliament passed the act transferring the payment of first-fruits of benefices, ecclesiastical dignities, etc. to the king and subsequently the latter ordered commissioners to value the ecclesiastical possessions of his kingdom. The *Valor Ecclesiasticus* is a valuable record of religious institutions at this time. It shows that the college was very much dependent on the early appropriations of churches made to it. The tithes and glebes of 16 churches yielded over £200 for its benefit, while rents from farms and other land amounted to only £4. Allowed deductions were £1 to John Killigrew, auditor of the college, and 10s. to Stephen Gayre, its steward. Alms distributed yearly for the soul of the founder amounted to £3.12s.8d. Part of the income was expended as follows: the portion of the provost £32.18s.7d. (£24 for his prebend, 2s.2d. for his obit and £8.16s.5d. for his share of the common fund), of the sacristan £10.4s.7d. (£1.6s. for his prebend, 2s.2d. for his obit and share of the common fund £8.16s.5d.), of 11 canons £98.4s.5d. (2s.2d. for an obit for each and £8.16s.5d. each out of the fund), of 7 vicars £42.15s.4d. (1s.10d. for an obit and £6.0.4¼d. for stipends), of 6 choristers £5.8s. (6½d. for obits and 17s.5½d. for stipends), of the chantry founded by Thomas Brantyngham (1s.10d. for obit and £7 for stipend), of the chantry of Otto de Bodrugan (1s.10d. for obit and £4.7s. for stipend) and of that of John de Beaupre and Margaret his wife (1s.10d. for obit and £4.6s.8d. for stipend).

The record provided is a valuable one and gives useful insight into the college's establishment in its final phase. Perhaps it was a bit too neat and no doubt in operation, as the history of the place shows, the financial management was not so smooth and efficient as it might suggest. The return was not regarded, however, as detailed enough and in November a further compilation was made. In this was listed the names of the provost James Gentle, a new sacristan Robert Bodye, and twelve prebendaries as well as the common possessions of the college, amounting in value to £165.18s.7½d., which was 'applied to the daily maintenance of the resident canons, vicars choral, clerks of the second form, choristers, and other ministers serving God'.

Not long after this there is another record of the college, though viewed from a different approach. John Leland visited Cornwall in 1538 and gave this account of Penryn and Glasney:

The first Creke or Arme that castith out on the North West side of Falemuth going up perin, and at the Ende it brekith into 2 Armes, the lesse to the College of Glasenith, i.e. viridus nidus or Wag Mier at Perin, the other to S. Gluvias, the Paroch Chirch of Penrine therby. Peryn a prety Towne of Marchandyse and Vytayle Market. Yn the Town ys a Chapel, and a Quarter of a Myle out of the Town ys the Paroch Chyrch. Stakes and Foundation of Stone sette yn the Creeke at Penrine afore the Town, a little lower then wher it brekith into Armes, a Gap in the Midle of the Stakes and a Chain. One Water Goode, Bisshop of Excestre, made yn a More, caullid Glenith, in the Botom of a Park of his at Penrine, a Collegiate Church, cawled S. Thomas, wher be Secular Chanons with a Provost, twelve Prebendaries, and other Ministers. This College is strongly wallid and incastellid, having three strong Towers and Gunnes at the But of the Creke. Good wood about the South and West syde of Penrith. . .

A map of south Cornwall at about this time indeed shows Glasney much as he describes: two round towers with in the middle a square-towered gatehouse abutting the creek and behind them a church, interestingly with a spire, surrounded by an enclosing wall.

In about 1520 a Star Chamber action brought by William Carvanyon, the lessee of part of the bishops homefarm at Penryn, paints, however, none too happy a picture of the life style of the last but one provost. James Gentle, he said, was a 'a man of great covetousy' and

hath not only let the college to be in decay so that the service is not ministered as it hath been, but also hath taken the chantries of the same college into his own hand and doth daily occupy them to his own use. And Sir James Gentle and his servants be men of great pleasure, more like temporal men than spiritual, do daily use hawking and hunting and do not only tread and break down hedges, corn and grass of them that be his poor neighbours there nigh him but also doth kill and slay with his spaniels, some days two sheep, some days three and divers times five in a day, and also do kill, drink and joust. . .Sir James is a man of great substance and being well friended, your poor orator can have no redress. . .

It was customary to lay it on thick in these cases but the charges have a ring of truth about them. Who but the farmer of the adjoining bishop's demesne would have suffered from the provost's marauding spaniels? As a social equal of the local gentry it is to be expected that the provost engaged in such pursuits as hawking and hunting; William de Bodrugan in the late thirteenth century certainly did. Indeed, this was probably much like the life style of the provosts through all of its near three hundred years of existence, with the ministrations of the church left to lesser officials. William Carvanyon no doubt knew that his allegations would have an interested audience at this time when the monastic establishments were on the defensive and Henry VIII's government was looking for ammunition to justify their removal.

A visitation of 1542 confirmed, however, that the buildings were in a state of disrepair; built in a marshy area, its lead roofs and timbers were in imminent danger of collapse. Master James Gentle's tenure of the provostship came to an end in 1546 with his death. He was succeeded by Master John Libby, who was instituted on 30th September by the bishop's commissionary general at Thorverton, Devon. He was the last provost of the college, now called St Mary's of Glasney. Henry VIII's aversion to St Thomas is also seen in the surviving cartulary of Glasney where the name is regularly erased or written over. Having dissolved the larger and smaller monastic houses, he now turned his attention to the chantries, among which Glasney was included as a college. In 1546 he caused a valuation to be made of the ornaments, jewels, and bells of these institutions and at Glasney, testifying to its former wealth and prestige, they were said to be worth the large sum of £153.0.8d.

The death of Henry VIII brought little change in the government's reforming zeal and under Edward VI and his uncle Somerset a new Chantries Act was passed which annexed more ecclesiastical endowments to the crown, more particularly lands given for anniversaries, obits, lights before images, etc. Commissioners were appointed to examine such holdings and in the winter of 1547-8 Sir William Godolphin, John Grenville, and Henry Chiverton made a tour of Cornwall's colleges, chantries, and guilds for this purpose. Glasney college they found to be much the largest foundation, in fact little less valuable than the largest monastic establishments in Cornwall, which had already been dissolved. Their report was quite favourable towards the college and its last provost. John Libby had done his best to make repairs to the buildings, having spent £40 to that end during the previous year, the church 'by reason of the open standynge of the same upon the see, by tempest of whether felle into suche decaye'. They noted that Master Libby was 'a man well-learned' and that this was 'a mete place to establyshe a learned man to teache a gramer schole or to preache Gods worde, for the people thereabouts be very ignoraunte'. The bellringer was paid 'as well for teaching poor men's children their ABC as for ringing the bells'. Earlier, one of the vicars who had acted as a schoolmaster had died 'for the which the people maketh great Lamentacione'. The importance of the college for the defence of the area was noted: the 'fayr havyn named Falmouth to which sometimes resort one hundred great ships, which being there have always used to resorte to the said Colledge to see the Mynystracon, and the walls of the said Colledge on the Southe-syde well fortyfied with Towers and Ordinaunce in the same for the Defence of the said towne and the ryver comynge to the same, whych Ordinaunce perteyn to the men of the said towne'. Also its value as a place of worship: 'This Colledge standeth Dystaunte from the parishe Church half a myle and more, whyche parishe Church ys very lytle for the nombre of the People in the said towne'. Elsewhere this was stated to be 400, 600, and even 1200 'houseling people'.

When the commissioners were there the establishment consisted of John Libby the provost, aged 60, and seven resident prebendaries aged 70, 70, 60, 45, 46, 80, and 45. There were three non-resident canons and two other places were vacant. The four choristers were children, aged 10, 12, 13, and 12, and there were also seven vicars, a chapel clerk, the bellringer, and three chantry priests. The yearly value of the lands and yearly profits pertaining to the college, including $5\frac{1}{2}$ acres of wood, possibly adjoining Bishop's wood, amounted to £228.3s.7d. Plate and jewels weighing 493oz., gilt 210 oz., parcel gilt and silver 283oz., made up the ornaments which were valued at £26. Lead on the roof amounted to 40 foder, of which 8 foder had already been taken away for the use of the fortifications on the Isles of Scilly.

But efforts were still being made to save the college, if not for the purpose of establishing a grammar school (though Penryn in the seventeenth century was to get a Latin school, something similar), for it to be converted into a parish church. Early in 1549 it was said 'proceedings are now being taken by certain gentlemen of the county, to have the sale cancelled and the church (which has already been in great part dismantled) converted into a parish church'. However, they were unavailing and the materials of the college were sold in December to one Giles Kelwaye: five bells from the steeple weighing two tons £40, a small bell called the marowmasse bell from the steeple weighing one hundredweight £1, the remaining lead from the roof £88, stones and timber from the church, the cloister, and steeple £20; in all £149.

Also disposed of were the vestments, cloths and books. A long list of these is recorded in the state papers which are believed to have come from Glasney. Their details give a vivid impression of the former style of the place. Four copes, one of 'green velvet and cloth of gold written upon the cope "Pray for the soul of John Bishop" ', two of 'crimson and velvet and cloth of gold caped and bordered about with green velvet and cloth of gold', and the other of 'crimson damask and gold caped and bordered with green velvet and cloth of gold'. There were ten vestments. One of 'crimson velvet and cloth of gold' with on the cross the back the resurrection depicted; another similar, with on the back the words *Vero filius dei erat iste*; one of 'cloth of tissue, green and red velvet, on the cross on the back, St James and on the breast St Peter'; another similar with Christ depicted on the back and Our Lady on the front; one of 'crimson damask and gold' having the passion of Christ depicted on the back and St James on the front; one 'of green branched and spangled and bordered about with crimson velvet and gold and written upon the cross of the back *Ave Maria gra pena*'; another similar with on the cross written Elias; one of purple velvet with a picture of Christ nailed to the cross; one of the black velvet with drops of gold with the same picture, and the last of red satin *bryges* and green 'the word Jhue written upon the cross of the back'.

There were three vestments for deacons; one of crimson velvet and cloth of gold and upon the breast an angel with a sword in the hand, another of the same material and in the lower section St Peter, and the third similar with the picture of St James and the word Jacob written. Six altar cloths, two to hang 'before and above an altar of black velvet and crimson satin with the images of Our Lady, the roses and white lady embroidered'; two other pieces for an altar of white satin, gold, blue, green, and red velvet and three *panis* in them in gold with images; one other altar cloth of blue velvet with letters of gold and having in the midst a picture of Our Lady and her Son set in a tabernacle of gold with three other images; another of crimson velvet with three panes of cloth of gold embroidered with a white lion; one of green velvet wrought and written upon the same Ecce homo; two others of russet, white, and yellow satin. In addition there were seven albs, that is tunics of white cloth reaching to the feet, three of which were suitable 'to the best suits'; three tunicles (vestments with wide sleeves usually worn over the alb by subdeacons); eight stoles, two of them cloth of gold; seven sleeve hangers, three of them of cloth of gold and 'six other small pairs of divers sorts, three of them of cloth gold'.

Of other items the list included one cross of copper with a pair of cruets, three books 'whereof one is an old written primer' and 'two portasses [portable breviaries] of the persons of Borley', a tabernacle with an 'image within the same having a cross in one hand and a book in the other', 'a stained cloth having in the same the picture of Christ nailed to the cross with the picture of Mary and John', 'a little paper painted with the five wounds', another stained cloth depicting St Francis, a white missal, containing the service of Mass for the whole year, four large books of parchment with text hand-written in Latin and a little gilded bell with a handle of crimson silk and gold. The items give very well an idea of the scale of the church with its many priests and frequent services.

As for the residents at the closure, they received pensions; John Libby the provost £18.7s.1d. yearly, five canons £6.13s.4d., the other six £6, the two chantry priests £4.12s., the chapel clerk and bell-ringer £2, while smaller pensions amounting to £10.11s.4d. went to lesser personages. So concluded with an abrupt finality the religious house that had been a premier influence through west Cornwall for nearly three centuries. There can be little doubt that resentment at its suppression played its part in rallying support among Cornishmen for the rebellion that occurred later in the year, which has become known as the Prayer Book rebellion.

John Balsam, Rector. Blisland, 1410.

CHAPTER II

The Buildings

THERE are allusions to the buildings of Glasney in several texts during the centuries when it functioned as an ecclesiastical institution but no maps or drawings — apart, that is, from the sketch contained within the Cottonian map of south Cornwall in Henry VIII's reign, which may be an imaginative reconstruction in any case. If one works back from the buildings as they survived in the post-suppression years it is possible to piece together something about them as they existed in their heyday. A detailed investigation of the site today would no doubt show that there is more surviving from that era than one might expect. Parts of the canons' houses to the south of the close may well exist; certainly an adjacent mill does. The buildings around the gatehouse and defensive towers were on the site of buildings to the west of St Thomas Street and parts may still survive. A small piece of the wall of the church remains on the north side of the Glasney recreation field, the wall of which dates back to an early period. The field itself, now owned by the local authority, Carrick District Council, is an interesting survival. Clearly it was the close and burial ground of the college. No doubt it is because it was consecrated ground that it remained untouched in subsequent years.

The Revd. C. R. Sowell, writing in 1865, described the piece of wall and the arch it contained.

The foundations of the north side of the Chapel [i.e. the church] can be traced somewhat accurately; and at the north-east angle they are very massive and strongly cemented. Measuring southward about fifteen feet from this point, we find, standing in a garden and attached to the end of a modern house, a damaged jamb, with the two stones of a pointed arch — apparently of a window; and contiguous to this, partly worked out of the same stones, so as even to form a constituent portion of the jamb, is a small column supporting the rib of a groined vault. . . most probably it is the north side of the Sanctuary, or Lady Chapel, originally separated into bays by the shafting now in the garden of College House: in which case, the jamb before-mentioned would have stood on the south side of the east window of the north aisle. This may have been the Beaupre Aisle; and it appears to have been vaulted with stone, and also faced with squared stone internally.

A short report by S. Drew in 1824, however, said that no vestiges of the college then remained. 'When the Reformation took place, its revenues being seized, the edifice was suffered to fall into decay. It was entirely demolished in the days of Hals [i.e. 1700] except one tower, which continued for some time to survive the other parts of the building. But this was pulled down about the beginning of the last century, and a dwelling house was erected on the site. This belongs to Lord de Dunstanville by inheritance from the family of Pendarves. The greater part of the lands belonging to Glasney College, came after some time into the possession of the Godolphin family. These are now the property of the Duke of Leeds'.

Drew's account seems to have had much truth about it for when Peter Munday described the remains around 1650 clearly much survived. 'Here are the ruines of the famous Colledge of Glasney: the ruines of the Church and Steeple yet to be seen; many strong towers remaining yet entire'. And this is also the impression gained from the best surviving drawings of the remains, those of Lord Burghley and Sir Ferdinand George, Governor of the Citadel of Plymouth, dating from 1580. While clearly the latter may employ some imaginative licence, as a reconstruction of the college when it was in its heyday it is probably the closest we are ever likely to get using the historical material that remains.

From the maps C. R. Sowell claimed to identify the embattled towers and the church, the provost's house, the refectory, the dormitory, the almonry, and the detached infirmary with its court for the recreation of the sick. While not having his confidence as to the significance of the adjoining buildings, some observations can be made. In the cartulary and other records, reference is made to the gate and gatekeepers, the de Ponte chantry near Glasney bridge, the gardens planted by Bishop Bronescombe, houses at Glasney for Bodrugan chaplains, the provost's house, church close, the college table i.e. refectory, treasury, chapter-house, common hall of the vicars, cloisters, and the steeple.

The de Ponte chantry was associated with the bridge known as Glasney or St Thomas's that linked St Thomas street with Budock Hill to the south. The chaplains appear to have had residences close by or attached to it. In her in-depth survey of the archaeology of the area, Deborah Wingfield suggests that the bridge may have been of similar length to that still existing at Gweek, thus quite a long one. It clearly lay to the seaward side of the three towers: two circular ones at the ends and in the middle a square one which contained the gate and gatehouse.

According to the map of 1580, on the northern side of the towers and on a similar south-east/north-west axis was a large hall-like structure joining the east end of the church. This and a sizeable building on the south side of the western end of the church, both abutting the church close, are the only buildings, as far as these maps suggest, that could have formed the treasury, the chapter house, the refectory, and the common hall of the vicars. It is largely a matter of speculation as to which was where. The refectory was probably near a spring; at the centre of the close there was once a well but springs also exist up the valley to the west; this would point to the building on the west side of the church. There must also have been a washroom and houses of office, probably over a stream of water at its outlet, so these would have been likely to be in the building by the towers. Here also may have been located the dormitory and the common hall of the vicars. The treasury may have been in the tower of the church or even in a second storey room above the large entrance porch. If there were a second storey room, as the map suggests, the chapter-house may even have been situated here. At ground level on the church close side must have been the cloisters, clearly not forming a complete rectangle as was usual but just a covered area or walk linking the south side of the church with the buildings on the east and west. As for Mr Sowell's almonry, presumably he meant the building on the west side below the canon's houses, with its court around it. The gardens and orchard lay on the north side of the church, while the provost's house was presumably the largest of the group of houses on the south, the most easterly one. Houses for lesser servants of the college, such as chaplains, may have been near the college in St Thomas street; Deborah Wingfield shows that the area bounded by this street, Bohill and Broad Street, was also within the bounds of the college.

The church was modelled on Exeter Cathedral and who can doubt that Mr Sowell's synopsis is generally correct, the lay-out and the size much as he suggests. There is no reason to doubt William Worcester's measurements — two hundred feet in length and one hundred wide at the transepts, contrasting with similar measurements for Exeter Cathedral of about three hundred and forty feet by one hundred and forty, making Glasney about two-thirds the size of the mother church. References to the steeple and the spire on the church in the drawing of Henry VIII's reign should not, I think, confuse one. Steeple can as readily signify tower as spire, while the buildings depicted on the Cottonian map are stylised. The church no doubt had a large central tower like that of Exeter Cathedral and as shown on Lord Burghley's map. The tower would have necessitated considerable use of lead while much of the roofs were covered with 'stone named Slate in that Countrye'. Within the towers were the five large bells and the smaller marowmasse bell.

The interior, consisting of nave, choir, ambulatory, and transepts must have looked much like the cathedral at Exeter, though on a smaller scale. Having been virtually completed in the third quarter of the thirteenth century, it would have been in a similar gothic style. Bishop Grandisson has been said to be the 'second founder' of Glasney and it could well be that in his period there was substantial refurbishment of the buildings. Door and window surrounds in Caen stone still in position in neighbouring churches at Mylor, Mabe and St Gluvias appear to be of this period and while they may not have come originally from Glasney, though this has been suggested, the work may have been similar to that provided by Grandisson for the church and give some idea what its interior was like at this stage. Repairs to the buildings are periodically recorded and in 1404 among other things the choir was 'newly vaulted'. As was customary in medieval churches the interior would have been bare of seating, its floor possibly of compressed earth — 'the country' as Thurstan Peter described it; certainly rushes were made use of as a floor covering in the early fifteenth century. Churches were bright, colourful places in the Middle Ages and no doubt the walls were painted to illustrate religious scenes, in particular those connected with the twin dedications, St Thomas the Martyr and the Virgin Mary. Though there is no mention of it, it is likely there was coloured glass in the windows, particularly the east window, no doubt again with scenes relating to St Thomas and the Virgin. The high altar was at the east end of the choir and here, in contrast to the nave, furnishings would have been more elaborate, with stalls for the canons and vicars, a carved screen, and a slate floor under which burials of notables could take place. At the very east end of the church was an extension which was used as the Lady Chapel. According to the maps of 1580 the transepts doubled as porches from the north and south though inspection of the similar and still surviving collegiate churches of Crediton and Ottery St Mary suggest that the entrances may have been west of these. Mr Sowell believed that the ambulatory on the north of the choir became the Beaupre aisle and, if this is true, the Bodrugan chantry with an altar at the eastern end would have occupied the southern ambulatory. Here too may have been placed the Brantyngham chantry. Niches in suitable places were occupied by statues; there were images of St Thomas and St Michael, and before them candles and lamps would have regularly been lit.

Indeed, a definition of the sacristan's duties in 1334 reveals the disposition of lights in the church at different times. At great-double festivals seven tapers were lit in the choir; four around the altar, two on stands on the altar steps, and one in the corona suspended between the choir and the altar. Behind the corona a lamp was kept burning night and day, whenever the taper in the corona was extinguished, out of reverence for the body of Christ. In addition two large tapers were placed on each side of 'the great cross', presumably the one outside the choir and referred to in the statutes. On the principal festivals six tapers or candles around the corona were lit at certain services. Variations on the ways the candles were lit were observed for different festivals and services, while a light was kept permanently before the statue of St Thomas.

So much must be speculation about the lay-out of the buildings and how their interiors were made use of, and the only way by which clarification can come is by detailed archaeological investigation of the site. Let us hope that this will be carried out in the not too distant future. Meanwhile, careful observation and study of the remains that do survive, even down to single stones and groups of stones, would be useful and it is to be hoped that this too will be carried out.

Thomas Awmarle, Rector, Cardynham, c. 1400.

CHAPTER III

Officials And Daily Life

IN the earliest document that survives relating to the college, entitled *Ordinacio Canonicorum de Glasney*, dated 26th March, 1267, Bishop Bronescombe appointed thirteen persons to be instituted forthwith as 'canons secular' of the college. Each of them, either by himself or by a suitable vicar to whom 20s. was to be paid out of his master's portion, was to serve faithfully and continuously in the church. One of the canons or portioners was to be proctor of the college until the bishop, after conference with his chapter, should ordain otherwise. The first proctor was Henry de Bolleigh, who had held several ecclesiastical positions in the west of Cornwall before his appointment. He resigned the office in March 1276 but a letter from the bishop bid him to discharge the duties as far as they extended to matters of jurisdiction until a successor had been appointed. Apparently he had to wait some time for, according to Thurstan Peter, it was not until the appointment of William de Bodrugan on 17th April, 1283 that he was succeeded. Moreover, Bishop Quivil then formalised the position of provost, which before that time appears to have been a non-statutory arrangement.

In an ordinance of that date the bishop, drawing attention to the distance of the college from Exeter, which prevented efficient personal government and correction, with the consent of the chapter of Exeter, ordered 'the appointment of a provost who should be in priest's orders and should reside during two parts of the year, either continuously or at intervals, and was to exercise the same jurisdiction and moral government over all the canons and clerks of Glasney, in order that, as far as possible the daughter should imitate the mother'. William de Bodrugan was appointed the first provost and for his better support the church of St Probus was provided for him. As it happened, this arrangement did not work, as the church was already held by the treasurer of Exeter. However, the matter was sorted out in 1288 when Probus was acknowledged as the right of the treasurer and the provost was provided with Mylor in its place. By this time William de Bodrugan had resigned and on 28th February that year Walter de Fermesham, one of the founding canons, was confirmed as provost.

With the grant of Mylor to the provostship a more detailed description of the duties of the office was given. At the time of his institution the provost should hold subdeacon's orders at least and proceed to priesthood in due course. He was to be in residence for two-thirds of the year at a minimum. He was to have jurisdiction over all canons and clerks, with all necessary powers for the regulation of manners and the guidance of souls, in the same way as the dean had over the canons and clerks of Exeter. Walter de Fermesham who had 'for some time presided over the College with faithfulness and success, and had been called provost, to be so in reality'. He and his successors were to have the principal stall in the choir and seat in the chapter.

By his oath of office the provost swore on the gospels, with the utmost of his power to 'recall and reform to the ancient state long used and approved, the rights, liberties and customs of the said church, by whomsoever, under whatsoever colour or veil assailed, and so recalled and reformed as far as the laws permit' to guard and defend them with all his strength. He promised to be faithful to the church and Canons and not to reveal the secrets of the chapter. The services which he was especially called upon to celebrate were those of the main Christian festivals of the year, together with the dedication of the church to St Thomas the Martyr (27th March) and the obit of the founder on St James's Eve (24th July). As well as conducting religious ceremonies, the provost as head of the chapter was called to manage the general and secular affairs of the college. The statutes of Exeter Cathedral held sway but some individual to Glasney were also provided and added to from time to time to deal with special problems that arose. It was later said that these statutes were accustomed to be read regularly aloud before residents at the college to reinforce their message; in some colleges they had to be memorised completely.

The rules dealt both with religious and secular matters. Divine offices by day and night were to be duly celebrated in the church and the canons present and the vicars were daily to attend in the chapter to manage affairs appropriate to their section. The canons and inferior clerks were to show due reverence to their elders, on pain of standing before the crucifix outside the choir for one day and one night following, or longer, at the will of the provost and chapter. Obits of the dead were to be fully celebrated and one canon and one vicar to be stewards of the obits and to see they were strictly performed. Priests nominated to celebrate the perpetual anniversaries were to follow the procedures planned for the vicars on pain of losing a fortnight's stipend. For weightier business of the church, such as the letting of farms, presentation to benefices, the conducting of pleas and such matters, all the canons were to be given ten days' notice of meetings. Canons should not impede vicars in the execution of their offices by household duties. Two principal clerks were to be made proctors, with two deputies to see that peace and silence were observed in the church while meetings and gatherings were prohibited from it. Any detractors and sowers of hatred, encouraging schism and discouraging charity among the residents of the college, were to be immediately banished and excommunicated by the provost or his deputy without reference to the bishop; no canons were to receive the tithes of more than one farm at the disposal of the chapter, others were to be granted to him who offered the most (as rent for the right to receive tithes) and had made due residence; all monies due for farms were to be paid promptly to the steward of the exchequer, otherwise they might be deprived of the farms or punished as the bishop decreed; no canon, vicar, or other nominated priest was to enter the choir in secular dress after the sounding of the Mass of the Blessed Virgin on pain of losing the upper garment he was wearing, which was to be converted to the use of the proctors and boys of the choir. The statutes were to be duly observed, the penalty for trespasses being reserved to the bishop. Clearly some of the later ones had been added in the light of experience; the statute regarding proctors referred to the

Statute of Lyons of 1274 and the reference to schisms, no doubt, to the papal disputes of the late fourteenth century.

Following a disputed succession to the provostship, a commission was issued in 1375 to examine the position of the provost, and John Turall, vicar of Bodmin, held a court of inquiry. By the oath of several witnesses he found that the provostship was not a dignity, but an office, and had always been so reputed, involving the care and rule of the entire college. Some provosts had been permitted to hear confessions by the bishops but the cure of souls in confession did not pertain to the office. It was the opinion of witnesses that the provost had the same jurisdiction over the canons and other ministers of the college as the Dean of Exeter had over the ministers of that church, though from time to time the bishop had claimed this right for himself against the provost. He had no powers of visitation or right of procurations but could suspend vicars and other inferior ministers for misconduct in the choir and could fine them as the statutes allowed, but the business concerns of the canons and other ministers were outside his jurisdiction. The excesses of canons were referred to the bishop but inferior clergy could be corrected on the spot, though the bishop retained overriding powers to punish all excesses. Clearly it was a fine balance between the powers of the provost and bishop with the canons themselves retaining a certain independence. No doubt with determined or awkward individuals in office the balance could be and was disrupted, as the history of the college shows from time to time. The provost was always one of the canons and, like the Dean of Exeter, was always but one amongst his fellows, *primus inter pares*.

His role in the college was, though, a commanding one and he exercised an influential position in the community at large, also taking a lead in settling disputes, witnessing important charters at the college in connection with local land transactions, appearing on commissions and, like Sir John Oby, acting as a tax collector. Much depended on his character and the way he approached his position. Thus while towards the end of the days of the college, James Gentle appeared as a 'man of great covetousy' and he and his men 'more like temporal men than spiritual', he was succeeded by a much respected figure, John Libby, 'a man well-learned'.

Provosts, like other canons, were appointed by the bishops of Exeter and, while some Cornish connection may have been useful, the provostship in general appears to have been awarded to ecclesiastics whom they wished to reward or honour. It was also a way of exerting tighter control over the college. Henry de Bolleigh the first head was a clerk of the bishop. In the middle of the fourteenth century Master Richard de Todeworthe was a notary public and, with his non-Cornish name, may have been a legal associate or advisor. The provost who followed him, Sir Richard de Gomersole, had Devon connections with a prebend at Crediton and other non-Cornish interests and was for a time the steward of the bishop. Master Thomas de Walkyngtone, 1374-78, a professor of canon law, was a priest of the diocese of York and became chancellor of Bishop Brantyngham. However, he was too useful to the bishop and in October 1375 he received dispensation from residence as his master required his personal services. In 1377 he became Dean of Exeter, ending his days in the north, apparently his home territory, as Archdeacon of Cleveland. When a vacancy occurred at a time when there was no bishop, the king exercised the right of nomination. This was the case with Sir Reginald Calle in 1371 following the death of Bishop Grandisson and before the induction of Brantyngham. Here was another way in which non-local blood could be introduced into the running of affairs. Sir Reginald, as has been seen however, had a troubled tenure and died only three years later.

Some Cornishmen had been provosts in the early years, notably Sir William de Bodrugan, Master William Bloyou and Master Benedict de Arundell, but a distinct change in the character of provosts appears to have occurred from about 1400. From then onwards practically all had some Cornish connection; after all, for the smooth running of the college it was sensible to have at the head men who felt at home in the area. But they were not now men of the high gentry, such as the Bodrugans, Bloyous, and Arundels, but men from lesser families who had come up through the education mill; talented boys, who had clearly benefited from training in the local schools that were being established in the late

Middle Ages, and had frequently gone on to the diocese's own college of higher education, Exeter College, Oxford. It was all symptomatic of the religious, social, and educational changes that were taking place in the late Middle Ages. The establishment of a less strident, ambitious ecclesiastical leadership, coincided with the rise of the lesser gentry and yeomen of rural society.

In the early years provosts both before and after their tenure of office frequently held ecclesiastical positions of prominence in the south-west and elsewhere — this as well as any benefices they may also have held. Henry de Bolleigh was Dean of Probus from 1269, became Archdeacon of Totnes in 1275 and on resigning as provost became Archdeacon of Cornwall in 1284. In 1278 he obtained a prebend at Exeter cathedral. William de Bodrugan was Archdeacon of Cornwall from 1295 until his death in 1307 while Master William Fitz-Rogo was Archdeacon of Exeter from 1311. Sir Richard de Brayleghe, briefly admitted to the provostship in 1313, went on to hold various benefices and positions in Devon and in 1335 was elected Dean of Exeter cathedral. As has been mentioned, Master Thomas de Walkyngton went on to become Dean of Exeter and Archdeacon of Cleveland. Master Adam Sparke, Bachelor of Law, was official-peculiar in Cornwall in 1370 before taking on the provostship. Thomas Yorkflete, who is believed to have been provost around 1396, may have been the man of the same name who was Archdeacon of Berkshire in 1389.

After about 1400 careerist ecclesiastics did not play such a big part in the affairs of the college and more use appears to have been made of talented local men who had risen through the ranks. From that time all provosts were 'masters' or had clearly received some training at Oxford, save Sir John Oby; Sir like Lord being an honorary title for ecclesiastics who had not obtained such a degree. Many had been to Exeter College and some had achieved high position there. Master Walter Trengofe, Master of Arts, Doctor of Divinity, a fellow between 1403 and 1417, and from 1418 to 1420 chancellor of the university, was at some time rector of the college. Master Michael Trewynnard was a fellow of the college from 1429 to 1438 and for some years between 1436 and 1444 principal of Hart Hall, now part of the college. His successor, Master John Evelyng, was an MA of Exeter, a fellow betwen 1438 and 1451 and rector for a period. Master John Nans was a doctor of both laws at Oxford and went on to attend the University of Bologna, where he achieved the rectorship of both universities there. The last provost, John Libby, described as 'a man well-learned', clearly had received university training. Undoubtedly this change must have had an effect on the character of the college and its relationship to the local community. Leadership in the hands of educated Cornishmen, in their nature loyal to the land and its people, must have galvanised Cornish feeling in this outpost of the bishopric in west Cornwall.

Provosts of Glasney

Henry de Bolleigh 1257-83
William de Bodrugan 1283-88
Walter de Fermesham 1288-about 1296
Master William Fitz-Rogo 1296-before 1312
Sir Richard de Brayleghe 1313
Master William Bloyou 1313
Master Benedict de Arundel 1313-before 1328
Richard Seneschal 1328-at least 1335
William Heghes 1347
Master Richard de Todeworthe 1347-48
Sir Richard de Gomersole 1348-at least 1360
Robert Hoo 1370
Sir Reginald Calle 1371-74
Master Thomas de Walkyngtone 1374-78
Master Adam Sparke 1378-80
Sir Walter Myn 1380-83
John Edneves 1383-85
Sir John Raufe 1385-probably 1394
Thomas Yorkflete 1396 (?)
William Cullyng 1394-22
Master Nicholas Harry 1423-27
Master Walter Trengofe 1427-36
Master Richard Reddew 1436-63
Michael Trewynnard 1463-71
Master John Evelyng 1471-77

Master John Pascowe 1476-91
Sir John Oby 1491-97
Master John Nans 1497-1501
Master Alexander Penhylle 1501-07
Master William Uryn 1507-19
Master John Corke 1519-26
Master James Gentle 1526-46
Master John Libby 1546-49

The sacristan was an important figure in the affairs of the college. When a provost was to be inducted the mandate was usually directed to him or to the president of the chapter. The office appears to have been in existence from the commencement of the college though the names of early holders are not known. As has been noted, his principal duties were the care of vessels and vestments, the superintendence of the cleansing of the church, and the opening and closing of the doors and gates. It was not a popular office and there was considerable unwillingness on the part of canons to take it on in view of the responsibilities and small emoluments.

The sacristan was referred to in a charter of the bishop in August 1275 in which he and the provost, or one of them, was instructed to present two chaplains of the de Ponte chantry. The following year he was given charge of the revenues from the appropriation of St Colan church; these were to be used for the celebration of the feast of St Gabriel, the bishop's patron saint. In 1315 Bishop Stapeldon, endeavouring to see the work of the office properly carried out, gave permission to Sir Robert Tredowel to combine it with that of 'custos' or warden, although the holding of two offices by the same man was against the rule. In the Kalendar of Obits Sir Robert was described as the first sacristan and, though clearly others had undertaken the work previously, it seems that he was the first formally to be established in the office for any length of time. On the resignation of Otho de Northwode from his prebend Sir Robert was collated to it in June 1334, and Bishop Grandisson annexed the prebend to the office in perpetuity. Sir Robert's work must have been appreciated for 'many flattering epithets' were used by the bishop in his grant.

Bishop Grandisson's confirmation of the appropriation of St Colan at this time gives some idea of the multifarious duties involved in the office. At St Colan he had to collect the tithes and dues from the church, over and above what was necessary to maintain a vicar there, and to distribute the money to the vicars and the canons as ordained by the original charter. On the festival of St Gabriel he provided the lights at vespers, matins, masses, and canonical hours, as on Christmas day, and distributed 60s. in bread to the poor. He provided a clerk of the second form (in addition to those already serving in the church), who wore his habit in the choir and whose duty it was to sound the church bells and open and shut the gates of the close at the proper times, handing the keys of the gates after curfew to the sacristan or provost. He provided the bread and wine for the Eucharist and waxes and torches for the many varied services, frankincense, charcoal, mats, and straw for the whole church and ropes for the bells. He had the custody of the books, vessels, vestments, and other ornaments in the church and had to keep them in proper repair. Together with the provost he had to make sure that silence was observed in the choir and that proper pauses and stops were observed in chants and psalmody.

For the discharge of these duties he received from the provost and chapter at Easter and Michaelmas a total of six marks of silver, while all the wax that was offered at these times and the customary dues at the installation of canons were also his. On his initiation to his office he took the customary canonry oath; the same as that of the provost, except that he pledged obedience to the provost; and swore on the Holy Gospels to actually and continously reside within the close at Glasney.

The position of the sacristan and his relationship to the provost occasionally caused difficulties, and clarification of their respective roles was necessary. In July 1336 Bishop Grandisson established the periods of residence deemed necessary for the sacristan. He was to be in residence for at least three out of the four parts of the year, the four terms being from 30th September to 30th December, 31st December to 31st March, 1st April to 1st July, and 2nd July to 29th September. Other duties devolved on him from time to time. When the Beaupre chantry was set up he was to find the bread, wine, and lights for the regular masses to be celebrated and in recompense received 4s.3d. out of the fruits of St Just in Penwith, which Sir John had granted the college.

In 1379 a commission was addressed to the sacristan, then Sir Geoffrey Carew, who, with the official-peculiar in Cornwall, was to inquire into certain abuses at the college. There was clearly some maladministration in the office before 1387 for in that year it was found that certain ornaments, vestments, and other goods bequeathed to the church had been dispersed. On his visitation in 1400 Bishop Stafford ordered a tightening-up in the operations of the office. Through his clerk, the sacristan was to see that the ringing of the bells for services was carefully attended to, the closing of screens, gates, doors of the church, and the gate of the close carried out in good time 'lest damage happen to the church or scandal to its ministers'. He had to make sure the bread and wine provided daily for mass was pure and not acid and the vessels used at the altar clean. In case of negligence 'thrice repeated' the clerk was to be dismissed by the sacristan after a month's notice and a successor appointed. Part of the stipends of the canons were given over at this time to repairs necessary for the church; excepted though, were those of the sacristan Geoffrey Carew and John Raff, because they alone had no benefice outside the college. In the bishop's commission the sacristan was bound to perpetual residence and was to take the place of the provost in his absence and to dispense hospitality.

In 1424 a dispute developed between the sacristan and the chapter over the repair of books and ornaments. In August Bishop Lacy wrote to the Dean of Kerrier and Sir John Rawlyn, vicar-choral at Glasney, insisting that the sacristan, Master Nicholas Harry, obey the judgement of the commissaries. Master Harry was clearly a man of fighting spirit and stood out for the preservation and enhancement of the duties of his office. He claimed that no minister should leave the college without his leave; that at the great-double feasts he should lead in divine service, and that in the absence of the provost he be president of the canons sitting in chapter; when the provost was present he claimed the second place. These and other matters were referred to the arbitration of the Archdeacon of Cornwall, William Fylham, and a canon, Richard Olyver, and they in November 1427 gave pronouncement to a compromise: no one could withdraw from the college without leave of the sacristan; in the absence of the provost, the senior canon, and not the sacristan was to take precedence; as to the repair of books, etc., they confirmed the previous decision.

The position continued to cause problems. In 1447 the provost and the official-peculiar were requested to inquire into the deficiencies of the office. When in September 1451 Thomas Schanke was collated, he was shortly after given permission to hold another benefice, as well as St Mawgan in Pyder which he already held, 'on account of the poverty of its endowment'. Concessions as to his period of residence at the college were also allowed at this time. Little is heard of the office in later years and presumably these problems were eased. In March 1508, though, Bishop Oldham granted the sacristan the sum of 13s.4d. annually out of the fruits of Manaccan.

As dissolution approached, the office was held for a long period, from 1507 to at least 1534, by Sir John Chimmowe, betokening a stable and responsible administration. Thereafter several held it for short periods: Sir Robert Bodye for about three years (he was the incumbent in 1536 when his portion and salary was said to be £10.4s.7d.), George Plankney briefly in 1537, William Reskymer for a couple of years until 1539, John Warene from then until 1541, and Matthew Newcombe until at least 1545 and presumably until the dissolution in 1549, as he was then among the canons who was awarded a pension.

The position was clearly a key one and a good administrator could make all the difference between a contented college, performing a valuable service in the community, and a disgruntled one where resentments could fester. Length of service might be one indication of a successful tenure, while the record of obits in the kalendar might be another. Sir Robert Tredowel, listed in the kalendar as the first sacristan, held the office from at least 1315 to 1334 and was clearly remembered with respect. Benedict de Arundel, provost from the time that he was collated in 1313, resigned that office some time before 1328 and, though unusual, may have been sacristan after that, before his death in 1332. He was remembered in the kalendar as a sacristan, as also was Ralph de Arundel, who was collated to a prebend in 1311 and was still living in 1353. He may have held the position some time after Benedict and before the collation of Sir William de Tregoney in 1349. It was probably around this period that Roger de Ponte was sacristan — he was recorded in the kalendar as such but without dates. Sir William de Tregoney held the position for at least thirteen years and another long server was Sir Geoffrey Carew (1379-1401) though, as has been seen, he had his problems. Master Nicholas Harry was sacristan for twenty-two years in the early part of the fifteenth century before becoming provost and gives the impression of having performed his duties responsibly. A successor who, confusingly, has the same name certainly began his period of office in a disputatious manner but went on to serve for twenty-three years and seems to have turned out to be a good administrator. The next sacristans held their posts for longish periods; Sir Thomas Schanke 11 years, Master John Pascow 4, Thomas or James Keylewey 11 and Sir John Oby 3; which suggests, as does the lack of evidence of any notable disgrace or disaster, a stable period in the college's history, as does the long period of governance exercised by Sir John Chimmowe from 1507 to 1535.

Often the position was a stepping stone to the provostship, as though the hard work necessary to run the college was felt to deserve the honorary headship as a reward in later years. This was especially the case in the last century and a half of the college's existence. After a long period as sacristan, Master Nicholas Harry was provost for his last four years (1423-27). Master John Pascowe was sacristan for four years, then provost from 1476 to 1491. Sir John Oby was sacristan from 1479 and provost from 1491 until his untimely death in 1497. Master William Uryn, sacristan before 1507, became provost that year and remained as such until his death in 1519. It seems it was during this period that the college developed a more corporate spirit, less under the heel and dependency of Exeter Cathedral.

Sacristans of Glasney

Sir Robert de Tredowel *c*.1315-34
Benedict Arundel-some time between 1313 and 1332
Ralph Arundel-some time between 1311 and 1353
Roger de Ponte
Sir William de Tregony 1349-62
Sir John de Treuranou 1362+
Reginald *c*.1375
Sir Geoffrey Carew 1379-1401
Master Nicholas Harry 1401-23
Master John Burdet 1423+
Master Nicholas Harry 1424-47★★
Sir John Fowlere 1447-51
Sir Thomsa Schanke 1441-62★★
Master John Pascow 1463-67
Master Thomas Kaylleway 1467+★
Master James Calwey, resigned 1478★
Sir John Oby 1479+
Master John Carewe 1492
Master William Nicholle 1492+
Master William Uryn, resigned 1507
Sir John Chymmowe 1507-35
Sir Robert Bodye *c.* 1536 William Reskymer 1537+
George Plankney 1537   John Warene 1539-41
Mathew Newcombe 1541-*c*.1545

★possibly the same person; ★★probably served to the final dates;
Thurstan Peter gives greater detail.

Examining the list of canons and prebendaries compiled by
Thurstan Peter gives some idea of the class of men the principal
residents of the college was drawn from and the changes that
occurred during the nearly 300 years of the college's existence.
The names of 256 canons were detailed by Peter and it is
instructive to look at the backgrounds of canons, by sample, at
fifty-year intervals. Canons were collated on the appointment of
the bishop, but while it was he who made the appointment it is
likely that frequently he acted on the recommendation of his

officials, more particularly the Archdeacon of Cornwall and his official-peculiar in the area. Though in the late thirteenth century such higher clergy were often drawn from the younger sons of lordly families and careerist clerics who, through their talents or contacts, achieved noble patronage, the expansion of the universities and, the rising wealth and social position of the gentry led, by the later Middle Ages, to their being drawn from a wider social background and having closer relations with their background and area. At the same time the ways of the bishops changed. While in the early period bishops of Exeter viewed Devon and Cornwall as their particular fief, making peregrinations though their estates from time to time and staying for periods at their manor houses, from about 1450 they visited Cornwall rarely which made more scope for local initiative, when a more democratic administration began to surface.

Undoubtedly the lesser clergy at Glasney had an important role in the life of the college but the basis of its existence was indeed the prebends and those who held them. The provost and sacristan headed their number yet the collective view of the canons at their daily chapters must have exercised the dominating influence over many questions. Bearing on this is how far and in what number they were resident. A document of the early fourteenth century stated that there were four terms of residence and provosts elsewhere were enjoined to be in permanent residence for at least two-thirds of the year. The qualifications for canonical residence can have been little different from that of the head of the college. The qualification involved forty-six days' residence in each term and every day they were expected to attend the morning or greater mass and to take the principal meal in the refectory. At times they clearly did not fulfil their responsibilities and in 1287 Bishop Quivil noted that some of the canons were frequently absent. But it cannot have been an arduous life for them, with their individual houses and gardens on the south side of the close, and with servants to do their chores; admonishment was given them in 1400 not to employ vicars to do menial tasks. A main daily meal was provided in the refectory and opportunity was given for study; some are known to have had leave of absence to attend university; and for leisure activities — Bishop Stapeldon suspected that some with doorways onto his park were 'making sport with his game'. No doubt it was all a change from the duties most of them also had as rectors and vicars of adjacent churches and from which residence at Glasney may have provided welcome relief.

The make-up of the first batch of canons has already been examined. Several had close ties with the powerful Earl Richard of Cornwall. Other founding canons were established clergymen holding benefices mostly in and round the Fal estuary. In many ways the college then had the look of a clerical club for the notable and substantial clergymen of mid and west Cornwall — a vehicle in the area for the influence of the bishop and earl in the religious field, with economic and social overtones also. Little is known about the educational background of the founding canons but undoubtedly it would have owed more to the patronage and support of leading clerics and noble families than to university training. It was not until 1314 that Bishop Stapeldon established at Oxford Stapeldon Hall (later to become Exeter College) which then became a seminary for young Cornish talent entering the church.

By 1300 the prebendaries had changed little in character from the time of the foundation. Some founders indeed were still in residence, notably Walter de Bodmin, who is believed to be the same person as Walter Peverell. William de Bodrugan, a scion of the Cornish knightly family, was a canon at this stage and other local men were Walter de Menecudel, clearly the same man as 'Walter de Sancto Austolo in which parish Menacudel lies', who was also rector of Illogan and Master Robert de Hendre, a sub-deacon, who was rector of Lanreath from 1284.

Five other canons at this time, however, seen to have been non-local ecclesiastics whose links were with the bishopric at Exeter. Sir Roger de Draytone in 1284 succeeded John de Esse who had been Archdeacon of Cornwall, and Master Thomas de Brewlaghe, succeeding Sir Michael Lercedekne in 1282, was rector of Northam in north Devon from 1274. Sir Robert de Welewe replaced Master Nicholas de Tregorrec in 1284 while Master John de Middeltone, who was commissary-general of Bishop Bytton in 1298, may have been the same as the man who, according to Emden, had leave of absence to attend Oxford in 1302 and subsequently held a variety of ecclesiastical positions in southern and western England — though at one stage he had a claim to the rectory of Egloshayle. Master William Fitz Rogo, who was to become provost until his death in 1312, may have obtained his Master's degree at Oxford but for three years before 1285 was at the University of Paris. He held the rectory of Highbury, Devon from 1267 and later was a canon at Exeter. In 1311 he became Archdeacon of Exeter. All five had non-Cornish names and clearly owed their advancement at Glasney to connections with the bishopric. It could be that after the death of Bishop Bronescombe, the succeeding bishops, Quivil and Bytton, lacking his commitment to the college, tended to use the canonries as a means of rewarding or promoting colleagues and associates.

Glasney in 1350 was still suffering the effects of the previous year's plague. Five vacancies were filled in that year; William de Tregoney was collated as sacristan on 24th April, John Aldestowe succeeded Thomas de Crouthorne of Crediton on 3rd May, Stephen Pempel Henry Broke on 8th June, William de Carslake Master de Stokes on 10th September, and Master Otho de Northwode Master John de Bodrugan the same month. Noticeably, several of the newcomers were of Cornish birth and it could be that the disaster gave added impetus to the trend to find local candidates for the canonries.

There is little additional information about Sir William de Tregoney except that he had been coadjutor to the vicar of Crowan in 1326. No doubt he held a benefice in the vicinity and was obviously of local origin. On 24th April, 1349, he was collated to the office of sacristan and to the canonry and prebend annexed to it. Sir John de Aldestowe was rector of Ruan Lanihorne in 1340 but the following year transferred to St Mabyn. The patrons of both benefices were members of the Lercedekne family and clearly he was *au fait* with the Cornish knightly families of the time for earlier, in 1331, he had been one of the attorneys representing the interests of Sir Otto de Bodrugan when he made his pilgrimage to the Holy Land. Master Stephen Pempel was connected with the Tregrisow family and had the

support of the Bassetts; while only an acolyte he was instituted to
the rectory of Camborne, the advowson of which they held. He
had a distinguished career at Oxford and went on to become
sacristan at Bosham in Sussex, Archdeacon of Exeter and Dean of
Wells — in which cathedral he was buried on his death in 1370.
Master William de Carslake obviously had a university training
and was rector of Philleigh from 1340 to 1345. Shortly after
obtaining the prebend at Glasney he was collated to the rectory of
Newton Ferrers in west Devon. Apparently he held the prebend
until his death in 1379; he remembered the college in his will,
leaving the substantial sum of £20 for the new fabric of the
church.

Master Otho de Northwode was not of Cornish extraction but
had a long record of association with Cornwall. He was the son of
Sir John de Northwode, his mother being the sister of Bishop
Grandisson. In 1333 he had been collated to a prebend at Glasney
but resigned this the following year when he was appointed to one
at St Teath. He resigned from Glasney again in 1354 but was
collated to another shortly afterwards. In 1345 he became
Archdeacon of Exeter and during his career held numerous other
ecclesiastical preferments, including prebends at Bosham, Ottery
St Mary (here his obit was kept) and in Exeter Castle as well as
several benefices in Devonshire.

Of other canons in the 1350s, Nicholas de Pomeroy is
mentioned in 1358 as having recently held a prebend. He was
probably a younger son of the notable west country landed
family, whose base was Berry Pomeroy in south Devon and who
held lands in the Tregoney area and other parts of Cornwall. He
is likely to have been connected with William de Pomeroy, said to
have held a prebend at the college around 1340. Local knightly
families clearly were giving the college wholehearted backing at
this time and members of families like the Bodrugans and the
Pomeroys were becoming attached to it or were making
recommendations to it — such as the Lercedeknes and Bassetts.
Master William de Heghes had local connections and as a poor
scholar at Oxford University had been given one mark by Bishop
Stapeldon's executors in 1334. Early in his career he had held
positions at Bosham and Clyst-Fomison in Devon but

subsequently transferred to Cornwall, being at various stages rector of Lawhitton, Philleigh, and Stithians. On his death in 1362 he held a prebend at Probus as well as at Glasney. Master Adam de Lychefielde was obviously of non-local origin and in 1336 was included with others in a royal pardon, after they had been attached for interfering with John de Melbourne in his possession of a prebend at York. He had had a university training but after these early troubles moved to the south in the 1340s, being instituted to the rectory of Northam in north Devon in 1348. He was collated to the Glasney prebend about the same time.

A similar mix of local and non-local canons is in evidence in 1400. Master John Landreyn, of Cornish origin, had a distinguished career outside Cornwall before resuming connections with his native county in the 1360s. He was elected Cornwall Fellow of Exeter College, Oxford in 1344 and subsequently became a Doctor of Divinity and Fellow of Oriel College in 1360. In 1362 he was instituted to the rectory of St Mawgan in Kerrier — the patrons of which were members of the Whalesborough family. It was at this institution that he appeared before the bishop in unclerical attire, and it was recorded that the bishop enjoined him to appear in future in such tonsure and habit as became his Order. It could be that he was one of those great intellectuals, forgetful of everyday things and disdainful of superficialities. He went on to achieve great things, was a Doctor of Medicine by 1366 and Doctor of Theology by 1373. It appears that he had the ear of the heir to the throne for in the latter year, at the request of the Black Prince, he was granted licence of non-residence for three years. He was granted leave again in 1378 to attend the Archdeacon of Richmond in his illness. Among other preferments he obtained a canonry at St Asaphs, one at St George's Chapel, Windsor in 1376 (the same year as he became a canon at Glasney) and one at the king's free chapel in Hastings Castle. In 1380 he was a member of the committee of twelve doctors who approved the decree condemning the heretical character of Wyclif's teachings and repeated the condemnation in an attestation at Black Friars in 1382. As well as the canonry at Glasney, he also obtained prebends at Crantock and St Buryan, all of which he held until his death in 1409.

Another talented Cornish boy who made good was Ralph Rudruth. He attended Exeter College and was a Fellow in 1369. He was one of the two senior Fellows of Oriel College before July 1373 and in 1386 and 1392 was Chancellor of the University. He was rector of Grittleton in the diocese of Salisbury before 1395 but no doubt because the call of Cornwall is what it is, in that year he exchanged with John Grey the rectory of Creed and a prebend at Glasney. He exchanged Creed for St Columb Major in 1399 with John Fecos. In September 1400 he was licensed to celebrate in oratories or chapels attached to the houses of the gentry. He died in 1404.

Master Nicholas Harry, who became sacristan in 1401 and provost in 1423, was of a different breed and clearly developed a strong institutional loyalty. He had a university training and is presumed to have held a prebend at Glasney before being made sacristan. He was at one stage vicar of St Just in Penwith and held the office of penitentiary in the deanery of Kerrier. Sir William Tregos or Tregoys, obviously Cornish, was established as a prebendary in Endellion before 1380 and in that year exchanged it with Sir Robert Vaggescombe for the canonry at Glasney. In 1395 he was instituted to the rectory of Philleigh. That residence at Glasney was a desirable proposition is shown by his request, with three other local clergy who were also canons, for leave of absence from their benefices for a year that they might reside in the college. This was granted in 1404 though their motives may have been less than laudable. In 1372 Bishop Brantyngham wrote to the provost, complaining that some rectors absented themselves from their parishes and resided in the college where they consumed the provisions and were a greater burden to the college than honour to God. They had been warned to return to their own churches within seven days, and in case of disobedience the fruits of their churches were to be sequestered.

Others in 1400 do not seem to have had initial local connections. Richard Hals had a Devon background as the son of John Hals, a justice of the King's Bench. His brother, also John Hals, became Bishop of Coventry and Lichfield. He probably had a university training and obtained a canonry at Crediton in 1392.

He was a great one for moving around and exchanging benefices, but for a time he held the rectory of St Ive. His stay at Glasney was a short one; he obtained the canonry in 1399 and resigned the following year. He went on to become a canon of Wells and also of Exeter and from 1400 was treasurer at the latter cathedral. He was a king's clerk and in 1414 was employed as an ambassador to Brittany.

John Hesylle originally held a canonry at the collegiate church of St Mary, Leicester but obtained a prebend at Glasney by exchange with Sir William de Feryby. He was instituted to Jacobstow in 1392 and several years after obtained leave of absence to reside at the college. He obviously built up a strong loyalty to the place and continued a canon until his death, some time before 1435. Benedict Canterbury, a Bachelor in Decrees, was instituted in 1395 in succession to Simon Wythiel, the patron being the king, during the vacancy of the see. His name suggests he was of non-local origin but he did have some Cornish connection, holding a prebend at Probus before 1387. In that year he exchanged this for the rectory of Camborne. In 1395 he became official-peculiar in Cornwall and in 1400 the bishop wrote to him directing him to inhibit a fellow canon, Nicholas Stoke, from cutting down timber in the woods of Glasney. His long tenure of the Camborne rectory — until his death in 1426 — and his position as canon of Glasney, also held until his death, suggests he also became firmly part of the Cornish scene.

Another likely non-Cornish canon at this time was Nicholas Stoke, referred to above. He had exchanged the rectory of Faringdon in Berkshire with the vicarage of North Petherwin on the Cornish border in 1372. In the 1390s he held the rectory of Stokeclimsland — the patron here was the Duchy and with his early post in Berkshire it would suggest he had connections with the Duchy household. In 1399 he exchanged this rectory with that of Withiel and a canonry at Glasney. In 1400, as mentioned, he was accused of cutting down timber in the woods 'without real necessity'. In 1402 he exchanged his canonry and the rectory with that of Hampton Meysey in Worcestershire. Later in the year he moved to Combe Martin in Devon. He was clearly not a settled person and failed to establish rapport with the Cornish. A man with whom he had contacts who was also a short stayer was Richard Noreys, who became a canon at Glasney in 1400. He had a university training and became a chaplain and rector of Combe Martin in 1392. In 1402 he gave up the canonry and exchanged with Nicholas Stoke, moving to Hampton Meysey.

Walter Estcolme was another man who moved into Cornwall though retaining a base in Devon. He was a Fellow of Exeter College in 1357 and 1358. Like numerous clergy at this time he became a pluralist, holding at the same time the vicarage of Sevenoaks in Kent, the rectory of St Stephen's, Exeter, from 1373, and the vicarage of Gwennap from 1377. In 1381 he exchanged the last for a prebend at Glasney. He gave up Sevenoaks in 1388 for the rectory of Stoke Damerel in Devon and it was as rector here that he died in 1410. Clearly he had not given his canonry the attention it warranted for after his death a commission was issued touching the delapidations caused by his neglect.

Talent and/or good connections continued to be key factors for obtaining prebends at the college in the mid-fifteenth century. Local men making good regularly figured as canons. Master Thomas Merderdewa, Master of Arts, was instituted to a canonry in 1447 on the resignation of Master John Udy. He was a brother of Master Reginald Merderdewa, rector of Redruth, who had done well in the church in Cornwall and elsewhere. Master Thomas was a canon of Crediton before moving to Glasney and subsequently was rector of Ruan Minor. His brother bequeathed him a gown and hood in his will of 1448. Sir Alexander Trembrase, a chaplain, was a canon at this period. No doubt he was related to Master John Trembras who died as parson of St Michael Penkivel in 1515 and whose brass survives. He was instituted as rector of Illogan in November 1435 and in 1449 while still there was on a commission regarding the patronage of Camborne, with Thomas Mate of Paul and William Hoygg or Hoggy of Gwinear. The latter was also a canon and had been collated to Gwinear in 1438. He held the benefice probably until 1462 when he was instituted to Redruth. His long service in west Cornwall betokens an interest and connection with the area though he may be the same as the William Hogg who was ordained deacon in 1431 on the recommendation of Rewley Abbey, Oxford.

The background of some canons may have been Devonian rather than Cornish. John Rowe or Rawe was educated at Exeter College and became a fellow in 1426 and rector in 1433. He was collated to the rectory of Farringdon in Devon in 1437 and became Subdean of Exeter from 1441. He was a canon of Exeter and rector of Exminster before being instituted to a canonry in 1449, when a chaplain. He died in 1463. One of his executors Sir Martin Dyer, also a chaplain, had become a canon in 1448. He resigned, however, in 1450. He was at one time a notary public in Devon, and was a canon of Exeter at his death in 1464. Master Henry Huchyn had a university training and was ordained priest in 1417 on the recommendation of Littlemore Priory, Oxford. He was rector of Sampford Courtenay in Devon for a long period from 1419 and obtained the canonry at Glasney in 1445. In 1447 he became rector of an Essex parish but thereafter his interests shifted to Cornwall; he was rector of Creed from 1448 and of Lanteglos by Camelford from 1452. He gave up Sampford Courtenay in 1453 and died not long afterwards. Master John Nicholle, Bachelor of Laws, like Huchyn, was instituted to a canonry in 1446 and retained it until his death in 1461. He was probably the man of the same name who held the benefices of Barnstaple and Stoke Rivers in Devon at this time.

The provenance of Thomas Abdy and Sir John Hynde, who were also canons in 1450, is not known though their names do not sound Cornish. Little more is known about them and the same is the case with Sir Thomas Messynger and Master John Gele, Doctor of Decrees, who was instituted in 1446. Again their names were not typically Cornish and they may have been non-local. Master Robert Aiscoghe was probably the ecclesiastic who obtained highest preferment outside Cornwall. He was Warden of King's Hall, Cambridge between 1431 and 1463. Before 1447 he was Archdeacon of Colchester and was then collated to the archdeaconry of Dorset. From 1458 he held a prebend and subdeanery at Lincoln and died there in 1471. He was possibly a relative of William Aiscough, the bishop of Salisbury who was murdered by the followers of Jack Cade in 1450.

If the non-local element was still quite large in the middle of the century, the process of making the college truly Cornish continued in 1500 as a natural and logical development, because the Bishop of Exeter tended to lose interest in his Cornish estates and became more embroiled in concerns in and round his cathedral city and for that matter in archiepiscopal and governmental matters. The college in west Cornwall naturally attracted people with the necessary qualifications who lived in or were of the area. The result was an intensification of interest in things Cornish, the Cornish background and culture and the fortunate creation of some of the main survivals of literature in the Cornish language.

A majority of the canons who were likely to have been of the college in 1500 were Cornish and others possibly were. The provost Master John Nans whose career is mentioned earlier certainly was; as well as holding a variety of positions outside Cornwall, he was at various times vicar of Gwennap and St Gluvias and rector of Camborne and Redruth. Master John Trefuthane was at the college in 1492 at the time of Robert Sherborne's visitation, being then described as a resident canon. He was vicar of Mullion until his resignation in 1512 and died in 1517. Sir John Knebone is likely to have been local. It is believed he was instituted in the early 1480s and continued as canon until his death in 1540. Richard Carlion was instituted in the same period and held his canonry until resignation in 1541. He also held the benefice of St Andrew's, Stratton, which he resigned the same year. No doubt he was a relative of John Carlion, the prior of St Stephen's, Launceston in the early sixteenth century, who held the patronage of St Andrew's. Master Alexander Penhill, rector of Illogan from 1493, was instituted in 1495 and went on to become provost in 1500. Master James Trevethan was instituted in 1498 and was another long holder of the office, continuing until his death in 1547. Master John Carew, a bachelor of laws, held a Dorset rectory first but became rector of Phillack in 1476 and of Lanreath the same year. He was a canon of Glasney from 1479 and was briefly sacristan in 1492. On his resignation in 1500 he was succeeded by another Cornishman, Sir Richard Fawey, chaplain, who held the prebend until his death in 1512.

Possibly Cornish, but his origins are not known, was Sir William Piers who was a canon until his death in 1505; described as Master William Pers in 1492, he was then non-resident. The backgrounds of Master Philip David and Nicholas Smythe are likewise not known. The former held a canonry until his death in 1505. The latter was instituted between 1480 and 1486 and continued a canon until his resignation in 1538. Sir Hugh Lynke, a chaplain, instituted in 1492, does not sound very Cornish. He was recorded by Robert Sherborne as non-resident and presumably was still holding his prebend in 1500.

At the time of the suppression the number of canons was somewhat reduced, two being vacant, and in the nature of things the calibre of those holding prebends may not have been what it should. Even so, the Cornish element in the college continued to be dominant. Master John Libbe was then provost, having been presented by John Grenville 'by reason of a grant by the bishop'. The Grenvilles were an important west country family with lands in north Cornwall and though Libbe's background is not known it seems likely he was either from Cornwall or Devon. The name, more commonly Libby, is not a rare one in the south west.

Most of the other men likewise appear to have been local. Ralf Trelabys or Trelebs was a canon in 1535 and was still at the college at its suppression, then aged 70. Thomas Vivian, also 70, was possibly the same as the Vivian who was a Fellow of Exeter College between 1511 and 1520 and, as an M A was instituted to the vicarage of Bodmin in 1516. He was a brother of the prior of Bodmin, also Thomas Vivian, and was involved in the latter's dispute with the town there. He was instituted to the canonry in 1535. Little is known about 60-year-old Mathew Newcombe and 45-year-old Matthew Broke but Gerens Johns was obviously Cornish. Aged 46, he no doubt had some connections with Gerrans parish. He was instituted in 1541, on the resignation of Richard Carlion, and at the same time was granted the benefice of St Andrew's, Stratton which had also been Carlion's. John Harrys, aged 80, had long connections with Cornwall. He was a Bachelor of Laws and had been instituted to Gulval in 1513 on the presentation of the Prior and Convent of St Germans. He obtained the prebend at Glasney in 1535 and in 1540 was collated to Gwinear, dying at the end of 1557. Nicholas Nicholls, 45, was instituted 'but one day before our comynge to take the survey there', according to the commissioners' report.

The three non-residents also appear to have been local. Henry Kyllyfree or Sir Henry Kyllyvreughe as he is described by Thurstan Peter was instituted in 1527. He exchanged a prebend with John Harrys in 1535 and the same year was instituted to the rectory of St Columb Major on the presentation of Sir John Arundell. He appears to have died or retired around 1550. Thomas Molesworth may have been the same as the John Mollswurthie, clerk, instituted to a prebend in 1544. John Molesworth attended Magdalen College, Oxford and became a lecturer and dean at the Univerity. He was rector of Week St Mary from 1509, of Stowford in Devon from 1511 and of St Mawgan in Meneage in 1526. It seems likely that they were one and the same person. Rauf Coche, a non-resident canon at the suppression was probably the same as Philip Couche, clerk, who was instituted in 1547. The incorrect Christian names used by the last two in 1549 may have been a little act of defiance by them when the survey was made prior to suppression.

The canons formed the basis of the college's existence, as spiritual fathers were central to its purpose and functions. In the 270 years of Glasney's existence able and talented men from Cornwall and further afield were provided with prebends and these men gave added strength to its ministrations and its standing in the life of the area. The college was a focus for the hopes and aspirations of able ecclesiastics, young men who had taken up careers in the church — which indeed was the main vehicle for the intellectually ambitious at the time. Noticed by clerics of the area or representatives of the bishop and with the support of gentry and knightly families, the usual course for them was to go to Exeter College, Oxford, for training. Subsequently they might join a priory or other monastic establishment or obtain a benefice. If not initially, certainly in due course many returned to their native land and if they were fortunate secured a place at noted Glasney. The fourteenth century saw increasing numbers of sons of the gentry, lesser gentry, yeomen, and tradespeople entering the church and using the promotion ladder in this way.

In its later stages there was an overwhelming Cornish presence at
the college and clearly towards its end it was a centre of
vernacular pride.

Canons held a variety of positions in the activities of the
college. Presidents of the chapter seem to have had some
independence from both the sacristan and the provost,
demonstrating the importance of the assembly of canons in
running the affairs of the college. Some difference in the authority
of the canons can be inferred when one reads that in 1400 a
majority of the seniors were to have the final say in the use of the
seal. One of their number also was called on to be a locum tenens
when there was a vacancy in the provostship. In 1435 two were to
be custodians of the keys of the chest that contained all moneys
and the seal of the college. The existence of a treasury shortly
after indicates that one of them functioned as a treasurer. With
their individual houses on the south side of the college, frequently
holding benefices and other ecclesiastical positions outside, theirs
was an attractive life-style. They had periods of non-residence,
but that it was an attraction for middle-class members to be at the
college is shown by periodic requests to have leave to reside there
and be absent from their benefices.

Just as in the television programme 'Upstairs, Downstairs'
where the impression is given that it was the staff below stairs
who created much of the character and ambience of the great
houses in the older days, it could well be that at Glasney it was
the permanent staff, the vicars, choristers, and the other servants
of the college concerned with its everyday functions who gave the
place its atmosphere and basic attitudes, and formed the way it
moulded into the life of the local community. The first thing to
appreciate about this under-life at Glasney was that the native
tongue was Cornish and that behind the scenes, in the sleeping
quarters, the washroom, the refectory, when at play or doing
menial tasks it was the Cornish vernacular that echoed round its
walls and rooms.

The vicars were established at the outset to perform the
religious services which were the basic function of the college. By
the initial establishment, the thirteen canons were each to have
vicars if necessary, to be paid 20s. annually out of their master's

portion who should 'serve faithfully and continuously in the said church'. Their oaths on becoming vicars speak much of their status: 'I. . .from this time forward will yield canonical obedience and reverence to the provost of the church of St Thomas the Martyr of Glasney, and I will be faithful to the church. The secrets of the chapter, to the damage of any member thereof, I will not reveal. I will faithfully hold blameless my lord [i.e. the canon employing him] by the due observance of the canonical hours, and I will be faithful to him in all things. Nor will I withdraw from this service without honourable warning of the provost for half a year before my withdrawal, unless it shall chance that I be promoted to a perpetual benefice. So help me God and these holy Gospels'.

The appropriation of the church of St Colan in 1276 to celebrate the memory of St Gabriel the Archangel brought some benefits to the vicars. Out of the fruits of the church each vicar was to receive 10s. yearly, while those who attended the services at the festival of St Gabriel were to receive 5d. in addition. The celebration of obits was another way in which the income of vicars was increased. By a charter of Bishop Bronescombe of 1272 he ordained that 8s. was to be paid yearly out of the college to celebrate the obits of the thirteen founders, of which 2d. was to be paid to canons attending the solemnising of each obit, each priest-vicar 1d., vicars of lower orders and clerks ½d. Eight shillings was the regular sum set for celebrating obits subsequently and presumably vicars and their inferiors received like sums when attending the services.

When Sir John Beaupre established his chantry in 1355 he said he had been moved to appropriate the church of St Just in Penwith because the vicars of Glasney were not receiving enough of their accustomed stipends. By his grant one of the vicars was to be nominated by the provost to say mass weekly for the welfare of Sir John, his wife, and relatives and they were to receive yearly of the fruits of St Just £4.6s.8d. divided amongst them. One of their number was also to say mass every day for the welfare of the bishop, the then provost Sir Richard de Gomersole, five named canons and a former canon, their relatives and friends and the faithful departed; for this another £4.6s.8d. was to be equally divided amongst them.

Vicars could be as guilty of neglect as their superiors and in 1379 an investigation was ordered into their 'crimes, excesses and negligences' as well as those of the canons and other residents of the college. In 1400 some were said to have absented themselves from the day and night services and to have 'scandalously' neglected their duties. The bishop laid down strict rules for granting leave of absence, which was not to be for more than a week or a fortnight at a time, or a month in the whole year. Moreover, lest it unbalance the singing and responses, too many from one or other side of the choir should not have leave of absence at the same time. Following an incident in the church in 1405, the provost, canons and inferior ministers were given licence to celebrate in the common hall of the vicars until there was a reconciliation. Shortly after, the canons were permitted to celebrate in their residences in the close, while the vicars and others were still to use their hall.

Only exceptionally was the rule waived that vicars had to be priests. In 1338 Robert de Tratherap, although only an acolyte or novice, received dispensation from the bishop to enable him to hold the office of vicar at Glasney at the request of the college. The bishop explained, however, that the concession was unique and was not to be treated as a precedent. Subsequently reference was made to the appointment of vicars-choral (in 1401), to priest-vicars and vicars of lower orders so clearly there developed some grading in the types of vicar; probably in the later period the college was unable to attract qualified men and some relaxation of the rules was necessary.

Their work was primarily the performance of religious services and ministrations; in 1400 canons were forbidden to hinder any vicar from doing his proper duty by imposing upon him any domestic service. As well as regular services, there were commemorations of the dead and private masses to be sung and recited. Care had to be taken that there was a balance of voices on each side of the choir so that in singing and responses there was a pleasing harmony. There were at least two stalls on each side, with the provost and some resident canons in the top right stall and another prominent canon in the left, probably the sacristan, with other resident canons. Below these came the vicars of varying degrees, clerks of the second form in the bottom stall and 'if there are any boys in the choir let them be set to stand on the floor of the church and be styled clerks of the first form'. Some of the minor offices were held by vicars, such as that of succentor or deputy of the precentor, the organiser of singing arrangements, and specificially mentioned in 1315, that of custos or warden.

They had their own chambers, presumably in the upper storey of the building linking the gatehouse and the church. In 1445 the bishop complained that the 'choir boys who had been accustomed to occupy a particular chamber in the vicar's quarters, had been deprived of their room owing to the neglect of the repairs' so they had been compelled to find lodgings in the town. As mentioned, they had their own vicar's hall — perhaps in the lower storey of this building — and in 1405 when the church was 'polluted' the bishop ordered services to be celebrated there until a reconciliation was made.

It is only rarely that vicars surface as individuals in the records. In 1313 a vicar of Glasney, Andrew de Penryn, was ordained priest at the distant parish of Kingston in Surrey by the Bishop of Winchester. Sir John Poghlande, a priest-vicar, in 1386 came to blows in the cemetery of Glasney with a Treliever man and in September of that year a commission was set up to investigate the matter. A vicar-choral, Thomas Trefuthon, helped organise the church's renovation in 1403 and the same year another, Thomas Chamberlyn, on account of his infirmity was allowed to celebrate where he was able in the college enclosure. A subdeacon, John Godegrave, was collated by the provost in 1410 as vicar of Sir William Tregoys who had neglected to provide one. In 1424 a vicar-choral, Sir John Rawlyn, was called upon with the Dean of Kerrier to secure a decision in the dispute between the sacristan and chapter. The unfortunate involvement of John Aunger, the vicar of the provost in the 1460s, in a case of abduction and legal conflict has already been referred to.

When Archbishop Morton's commissary, Robert Sherborne, made a visitation of the college in 1492 he found only seven vicars there instead of the statutory thirteen. They were Sir John Aunger, Sir John Higar, Sir John Chymmowe (later to become sacristan), Sir John Luky, Sir Richard Fowy, Sir William Breberveth and another, Sir John, whose surname is lacking. In his evidence Aunger complained that the statutes were not being publicly read and that their steward did not pay them what he received. Luky was said to be holding another vicarage while Breberveth, vicar of Gwinear, was told to reside there. There were also only seven vicars-choral at the college in 1536 and at the dissolution. In the first return they were said to be receiving £6.2s.2¼d. each as their portion, annually. Two places were vacant at the dissolution and those who received pensions then were William Knebone, aged 55, John Kylsye 35, Robert Morsse 40, William Hawton 50 and Robert James 30, the pensions being £7.10s., the same as their previous salaries.

The Penryn writer and merchant, Peter Munday, said in the mid-seventeenth century that his grandfather, of the same name as himself, was believed to be 'either Chanon or Chanter in that Colledge 120 years since'. No record of this survives but if his grandfather had been a vicar or canon he obviously could not have married. It seems more likely that he was a chorister who subsequently left the college and joined lay society. It is noticeable that the names of the few vicars of whom there are some details are mostly Cornish and it is probable that for the most part they and the lesser ranks of college society were local. No doubt it was good Cornish voices that sang the chants and recited the liturgies within the church walls of Glasney — the later expertise of the Cornish in choir singing may have been founded there.

Choristers at the college were sufficiently organised as a group to have a treasury as early as 1316 — as shown in an order of the chapter of Glasney for that year. In the *Valor* of 1536 six choristers were listed and as their portions they received annually 18s. each. By the time of the dissolution their number had been reduced to four — Henry Mychell aged 10, Thomas Wykes 12, Henry Couche 14, and Henry Goodalle 12. Their salary by then was £1 a year. Among other residents of the college were three chantry priests (discussed later in this book), a chapel clerk and bellringer. It is likely that as far as possible menial tasks were carried out by lesser members of the college though some aid may have been called in from neighbouring Penryn, if not on a daily basis, certainly when emergencies arose, such as major repair work to the church or other buildings.

It is clear from an interesting document drawn up by Bishop Grandisson in 1334 that the order of services at Glasney was much like those at other ecclesiastical establishments of the time. Reference was made to the celebration of matins, lauds, prime, terce, masses, sext, nones, compline, and vespers. In 1492 the provost, Sir John Oby, said that according to the statutes matins at Glasney were supposed to be said at midnight but this was being neglected at that time. Undoubtedly though, the members of the college rose at an early hour; at other institutions it was often between 2 a.m. and 5 a.m. Conformity with the general pattern may have been relaxed when numbers were reduced or discipline weak. In 1329 when justifying the appropriation of Mevagissey to the college it was said that the number of ministers at Glasney were 'too few for the proper services, especially for masses celebrated in the morning for the convenience of travellers'. The early offices, consisting largely of psalms, short prayers or collects, and versicles and responses including praises and intercessions, each with its appropriate reply, were regarded as preparations for the daily masses. The chief of these was the capitular mass, so called because it was part of the obligation of the members of the chapter to be present, the mass being sung by one vicar with the others in attendance. The vicars who had to celebrate obits or private masses in the chantries had probably completed these obligations by 8 a.m. or 9 a.m. and were able to break their fast, — unlike the celebrant of the capitular mass, or Eucharist.

Between the end of this mass at around 11 a.m. and the time for dinner at 3 p.m. the vicars were able to attend to their daily business. It was probably during this time that meetings in the chapter-house took place, also other tasks such as repairing books and vestments, choir practice, preparing the lights, and perhaps gardening, were undertaken. Meals were taken in the refectory when silence was observed, except for the voice of the reader at the refectory lectern, rehearsing some edifying work. During the latter part of the day some members of the college celebrated the offices of sext, nones, vespers, and compline which brought the day to an end. In some monastic establishments there was a different routine for winter and summer. In the latter with its longer period of daylight there was a main meal at midday, followed by a lesser one at 5 p.m. Silence was observed as much as possible, especially from compline until well into the following morning, and in view of the early morning services vicars and their attendants must have gone to bed soon after dusk.

Some details of the ringing of bells and lighting arrangements are given in the document of 1334. A bell was rung at the start of services and at certain stages during them. At matins a change in the lighting arrangements was made at the time of the second bell and the last bell. At the dissolution among the goods of the college was 'one litell bell named the marowmasse bell, wayeng 1 cwt'. This bell was rung for morrow-mass, the first mass of the day.

At vespers and matins on certain festivals, lights were kept lit until the last verse of the hymns at vespers, and at matins till the Gloria Patri of the ninth responsory and then the standard lights were lit by the altar and kept until the *benedicamus*, the blessing. On double feasts of greater solemnity the four standards were lit at the magnificat and *benedictus*, at lesser double feasts three. On major festivals, as Christmas day, the seven tapers in the corona above the choir were lit at vespers and mass and the three standards were kept until compline. Other lighting arrangements were specified for certain services when the invitatory, the verse of psalms introducing *Venite exultemus*, was chanted by three clerks.

At other feasts at which nine lessons were read, or three with 'rulers', that is, when led by the two principle choristers, a single light was lit in the corona, but at the magnificat and *benedictus* and at mass the standards were lit also. The rulers 'vested in amice, albe and stole and a cope of the colour of the festival' and each carrying a staff of silver or ivory, with which to lead the choir, stood in the open space in the middle, in front of the large antiphonary (the book of psalms) set open for their use. In the intervals they sat on moveable seats, placed near them for use as required. When necessary they moved up and down the choir; for instance, they stood before the dignitary who had to commence the psalms, etc. and gave him the keynote. There were variations in the number of lessons and psalms; on Sundays ordinarily eighteen psalms and nine lessons, on weekdays not being festivals, twelve psalms and three lessons, on festivals not being Sundays, nine psalms with three lessons. The latter were divided into sections, each being preceded by a benedication and followed by a response. For recitation purposes psalms were divided into seven portions and there were various arrangements for festivals that were not Sundays, when the psalms were sung without rulers. Lighting arrangements were enhanced on the feast of St Mary and after compline, at the antiphon, when verses of psalms were intoned by alternating sections of the choir, two or more additional lights were lit in the corona, according to the devotion of those willing to offer them.

The most important act of Christian worship, however, was the Eucharist or capitular mass. All partook at this service. The bread and wine was found by the sacristan who also supplied, according to the 1334 records, the wax, torches, frankincense, and charcoal. The latter two items were used for the high mass and at certain points in the service the incense was swung in a censer; its delicate blue smoke lifting gracefully heavenwards must have made a great impression on the participants.

As is clear there were variations in the services, from the greater double festivals conducted with the greatest solemnity, to the lesser double festivals, Sunday and weekday services, and single festivals not being Sundays. Especially important at Glasney were the services commemorating its patron, St Thomas Becket: the anniversary of his murder on 29th December, the translation of his relics on 7th July, and the anniversary of the dedication of the church on 27th March. St James's Eve, 24th July, was commemorated as the obit of the founder of the college, Bishop Bronescombe, while his patron saint St Gabriel was honoured on the first Monday in September. The bishop had a special affection for the archangel and his festival was celebrated in his time throughout the diocese. He made arrangements for a distinctive celebration at Glasney by the appropriation to the church of St Colan in 1275. On the day of the festival the sacristan distributed additional sums to the canons and vicars and solemn lights were provided at vespers and matins and at the mass as on Christmas day. At the same time he distributed to the poor of the area 60s. worth of bread. Other days celebrated with exceptional honour were those of St James the Apostle on 25th July, the Seven Sleepers (the seven youths said to have slept for several hundred years while in hiding from the Decian persecution) on 27th July, and Saint Michael in Monte Tumba on 16th October.

Deaths of important members of the college and benefactors brought special ceremonies in connection with the commitment of their bodies and mourning. Around 1310 Lady Sybil de Bodrugan is known to have been buried in the church before the altar, subsequently known as Bodrugan's altar. No doubt many of the provosts and leading canons likewise found their resting place within the church. Sir James Mychell, instituted a canon in 1435, in his will of 21st October 1438 expressed a wish to be buried before the image of St Michael the Archangel. On the night that a resident died it was customary for the whole community to accompany the body to the church, there singing all of the psalter as an act of remembrance. The offices of placebo and dirige were sung and the funeral of the departed took place the following day with committal either in the church or in the close.

Perhaps the most noticeable thing that people at Penryn would have missed at the dissolution were the sounds of the once living and celebrating religious community: for those nearby the singing and chants, coming over on the breezes, but above all the bells announcing the commencement of the hours and other services, and important phases in their celebration, and the marowmasse bell rung to announce the first mass of the day. When John Pownde rang the college's bells for the last time in 1549 it must have given rise to a deep feeling of emptiness in the lives of the people of this Cornish community.

CHAPTER IV

The Chantries

THE first chantry established at Glasney was the de Ponte, by Bishop Bronescombe in 1275. Referring to the insufficient number of ministers in the church of St Thomas he granted to the college the benefice of Minster, otherwise Manaccan, for the support of two chaplains. They were to say daily in the church the Mass of St Mary and another mass for the souls of the Bishop Master Henry de Bolleigh, Sir Walter de Fermesham, and all the faithful departed and they were to take part thereafter in singing the canonical hours. The chaplains were to be presented by the provost and sacristan and were to have as accommodation houses and outbuildings erected by the same Henry de Bolleigh and Sir Walter de Fermesham by Glasney bridge, i.e. adjacent to the towers of the college fronting the estuary. Their proximity to Glasney bridge no doubt gave rise to the name of the foundation, *de Ponte*.

Being presented by the provost and sacristan no doubt encouraged a close relationship with Glasney's administration. Roger de Ponte, whose obit came to be celebrated on 12th December, must have been an early chaplain of the chantry and was Glasney's sacristan for a time. Thurstan Peter's list of the chaplains of the chantry begins with Sir William de Coesgaran and Sir Nicholas de Spergor who were instituted on 19th March 1341. Thereafter there followed:

> *16th December 1357 Sir Nicholas Kevel, alias Bodewey
> 1st February 1363 John de Trevyda
> 16th December 1370 unnamed clerk,
>   probably Richard Tregaliseweare
> 11th August 1372 Sir Alan Trelesa

20th June 1393 Sir John Quynterel
29th May 1410, John Dawe
22nd December 1414, Sir John Godegrave
24th June 1435, Master John Burwyke
2nd January 1445, Sir John Ballam
2nd March 1445, Sir John Renolde
Before 1463, Sir Richard Boscawene
29th September 1463, Sir John Rynge
Before 1468, Sir John Gwyne alias Nicholle,
    perhaps the same man as Master John Nicholle
    instituted to a canonry on 26th April 1446
21st March 1468 Sir Richard Hygowe
July 1492 Sir Stephen Michell and Sir Odo Roby
    (Robert Sherborne's visitation)
5th April 1508, Sir Richard Tremanere
27th April 1513, Sir John Williams
Before 1534, Sir John Sawell
27th July 1534, Sir Henry Nicholle; described
    as Henry Trevarghe, alias Nycolle in the
    Valor of 1535
12th February 1541, Alexander Peryne
16th February 1545, John Chymmowe
    *specific days are those of institution

Some of the chantry priests clearly became quite important figures in the college. When under Bishop Stafford's instigation the members co-operated to aid repair work, it was Alan Trelas, Rector of the Chantry, who was appointed one of the two receivers of moneys and director of operations. In 1444 some doubt had arisen over the appointment of chaplains to the chantry and in that year the bishop issued a mandate to his official-peculiar in Cornwall to inquire as to its patronage. Being a chantry priest was one means of advancement for the aspiring cleric and was frequently an avenue to greater things. Some of the chaplains were canons as well, probably Sir John Gwynne alias Nicholle, certainly Sir Stephen Michell and Sir Odo Roby in 1492. The last holder of the chantry was John Chymmowe, no doubt a relative of the sacristan of the same name who held this position at the college from 1507 to 1535.

Unlike the three other chantries of the college, the de Ponte chantry was assessed separately in 1536 and was then stated to be worth £5.6s.8d., compared with Brantyngham worth £7.1s.10d., Bodrugan £4.8s.10d., and Beaupre £4.8s.6. While these occupied areas within the church, the de Ponte was clearly located outside, either in the buildings initially granted to it by the bridge or in the adjacent gatehouse. Like the college as a whole the de Ponte was swept away in 1549 and John Chymmowe was granted a pension of £6 a year in compensation.

The Bodrugan chantry was established in 1329 at the instigation of Otto de Bodrugan. The provost and chapter were to have the glebe at Lamorek (the old name for Mevagissey) and the great tithes of the main farms and in return 'admit a vicar in priest's orders, on the presentation of Sir Otto [de Bodrugan] and his heirs, in addition to the accustomed number, who should serve in the choir along with the other vicars, except at matins, and should, every day at dawn, at the altar known as Bodrugan's altar, where the said knight's mother lay buried, celebrate a mass for the souls of his father, mother and relatives of the said knight, and for his well-being during his life, as also for the souls of himself and his heirs after death, and at certain specified masses was to repeat a special collect with notation' — that is, sung to plain song, the Office Books being 'noted' for this purpose. To the vicar, the provost and chapter were to pay five marks sterling every year or, in case of depreciation, money to that full value. The vicar was to take the oath of canonical obedience in the same manner and form as the chaplains of the de Ponte chantry. Accepting C. R. Sowell's view that the Beaupre chantry occupied part of the north ambulatory, it seems likely that the Bodrugan chantry occupied the south. Otto had to find at his own expense books, a chalice, vestments and other such necessaries for mass and also houses at Glasney, all of which were to be kept in repair by the provost and chapter. Out of the endowment the provost and chapter were to celebrate the obit for Otto after his death. His obit was thenceforward celebrated on the 6th September of each year, which was no doubt the day that he died. The names of the chaplains who looked after the chantry are rarely known, but there is no reason to suppose that its ministrations were not well conducted for many years — the Bodrugans held the nearby manor of Restronguet and between 1342 and 1349 Otto's son Master John de Bodrugan held a canonry at the college.

Following the deaths of Otto's sons there appears to have been some loss of control and surveillance of the chantry. In 1396 a dispute over the advowson of the three chantries at Glasney: Brantyngham, Bodrugan, and Beaupre, reached the courts at Westminster. From this it appears that by then the rights of presentation had been amalgamated and were held by William Hankford and with them the manor of Keleyneke and rent from the manor of Lanistly. The marriage of the Bodrugan heiress, Joan, to the important Chief Justice from the south west, Robert Hull of Modbury, around 1405, seems to have encouraged renewed interest in the chantry. In 1407 Joan and Robert, in co-operation with her son by an earlier marriage, William, the Bodrugan heir, granted to Thomas Lessynwor, 'chaplain of the chantry at the alter called Bodrigannesauter', land at Trewithen, Probus, to provide for his maintenance and for the celebration of divine service for the soul of the founder of the chantry and the souls of Robert, Joan, and William after their deaths.

Apart from the clash between servants of Henry Bodrugan and John Aunger, vicar of the provost Michael Trewinnard (1463-71), the last of the Bodrugans, while possessing Restronguet and having interests in property at Penryn, seems to have had little contact with the college. He was on bad terms with the prior of Bodmin and though he made some religious donations he was clearly not the most pious of men. However, that the chantry maintained its independence in the years before the dissolution is shown by its separate assessment in the *Valor* of 1535. The portion of the chantry priest who held the foundation of Otto de Bodrugan then amounted to £4.8s.10d., of which £4.7s. was for wages and 1s.10d. for celebrating the obit of the founder. According to the chantry certificate of 1548 chantry priests at the college were then John Chymmowe aged 40, Thomas Michell 35, and Rauff Richard 30, the pensions allocated to them being £7.10s., £5, and £5 respectively. Presumably it must have been one of the latter two who was the last Bodrugan chantry priest.

The Beaupre chantry was established in 1355 as a result of the grant to the college of the church of St Just in Penwith by Sir John Beaupre. Two priests were to be received into the church over and above the accustomed number and were to be known as Beaupre priests. They were to celebrate masses for the well-being of Sir John and his wife Margaret during their lives and after their deaths for their souls and those of their relatives, ancestors, and heirs forever. They were to receive yearly of the fruits of St Just the sum of £8.13s.4d., divided equally between them. One of the thirteen vicars, nominated by the provost, was to say weekly a mass for Sir John, his wife, and relatives and for this the vicars were to receive £4.6s.8d. yearly divided amongst them. One of the vicars every day of the year was to celebrate one mass or requiem for the welfare of the bishop, Sir Richard de Gomersale then provost, Stephen Pempel, William de Heighe, William de Carslake, Sir John de Aldestowe, and William Tregoney during life and for their souls, and the soul of Master John de Stoke, a former canon, their relatives, friends, and benefactors and all the faithfully departed. For this the vicars were to receive an additional £4.6s.8d. every year divided amongst them from the fruits of St Just.

From the time of obtaining possession of St Just there were to be two clerks of the second form (who occupied stalls below the canons and vicars but above the boy choristers who stood on the floor of the church) to be called Beaupre clerks, who were to augment the numbers of ministers in the church, serving God and the church 'according to their degrees' in the day and night offices. They were to receive yearly out of the St Just income £3.9s.4d., payable at the rate of 8d. each weekly. There were also to be two choristers to be called Beaupre choristers who were to receive 4d. each every week, and one of whom was to serve the priests in the celebrations of the masses detailed above. The provost and the college were on the day of St Francis (4th October) to cause to be sung a mass with notation for the welfare of Sir John and his wife during their lives and for their souls after their deaths. It is to be noted that after 1369, by which time Sir John must have died, he was included in the obit kalendar of the Franciscan Friary of Bodmin, confirming his piety as well as his devotion to St Francis. In the Glasney kalendar his obit came to be celebrated on 24th August.

Bishop Grandisson laid down minute details of the times and nature of services to be performed by the Beaupre priests and the vicar deputed weekly by the provost, in the chapel of the Blessed Virgin, in the Beaupre aisle, believed by C. R. Sowell to be the ambulatory on the north side of the choir. Every day immediately at sunrise one of them was to celebrate a mass of the Blessed Virgin Mary; another, after the hour of Prime a mass of requiem; the vicar was to celebrate a mass of the day after the Sacrament of High Mass, except on major double feasts, on which days the mass of the day was to be said at tierce, in the chapel of the Blessed Virgin Mary in the Beaupre aisle. The chaplain who celebrated the mass of the Blessed Virgin Mary one week should the following week celebrate the mass of requiem and vice-versa. The two priests were to follow the said offices and daily hours as well as nocturns, like other vicars, except the one who celebrated the morning mass, who was also to be present at matins for that week. The bishop ordered that the two priests and clerks were to receive the distribution of obits like other vicars and clerks of the college. Sir John had to find for the said two priests books, a chalice, vestments, napkins, and ornaments and other things necessary for matins and masses and erect suitable buildings for their occupation.

The college had to wait eleven years before these arrangements were set in motion, until the death of Sir Reginald de Sancto Austollo in 1366, and Sir John himself had only a few years to see his scheme for Glasney come to fruition. The situation in the college appears to have deteriorated in the late fourteenth century and when Bishop Brantyngham made a visitation in 1386 he found grave excesses and offences. Money was missing; ornaments and vestments bequeathed to the college had been dispersed. He must have held the college in affection though, for it was during his episcopate that a third chantry was established; this became known as Brantyngham's chantry, and like the Bodrugan chantry was probably sited in the south ambulatory of the church. In 1393 he granted the college in his will 'his red vestment with the copes and other parts of the suit'.

By 1396, however, the rights of presentation to the three chantries were said to have been amalgamated and were then in the possession of William Hankford, along with the manor of Keleyneke (or Calenick) and rents from Lanistley. The latter was part of the Beaupre inheritance and obviously was related to that chantry. Calenick was certainly not Bodrugan land and was either something to do with the Brantyngham establishment or the Beaupre. There is little evidence about the progress of the chantries in the fifteenth century apart from the reinvigoration of the Bodrugan in 1407. At the time of Robert Sherborne's visitation in 1492 there were said to be at the college two 'annullarii', presumably chantry priests; Sir John Meub, canon, and Sir Ralph Harvy, also a canon. That the chantries retained their separate identities is shown by their separate assessments in 1536 — the portions of the Brantyngham being the largest of the three, valued at £7.1s.10d. (£7 for the stipend of the chaplain and 1s.10d. for the bishop's obit), compared with £4.8s.10d. for the Bodrugan and £4.8s.6d. for the Beaupre. In 1548 the college had three chantry priests; John Chymmowe, aged 40, was allocated a pension of £7.10s. and clearly he must have had charge of the Brantyngham chantry. Thomas Michell and Rauff Rychard, given pensions of £5 each, must have been the chaplains attached to the Bodrugan and Beaupre chantries.

Thomas Killygrewe benefactor of Glasney.

CHAPTER V

The Economic Basis

THE question has to be asked — how was it possible to sustain such a college as Glasney through all these years? The basis of it all was the exploitation of land by Cornish farmers, a little by exploitation of inshore waters by Cornish fishermen. The essential means was the age-old right of the church to take tenths of the produce for the maintenance of religious establishments by way of 'tithes' and by other exactions. It was by the appropriation of the income of churches to the use of the college that it was essentially maintained.

The usual pattern was for the bishop to appropriate the rectory of a parish to the college which appointed a vicar to perform the religious offices necessary there, supported by the lesser tithes while the college creamed off the major tithes and profits. Sometimes the major tithes were put out to farm and the farmer paid the college so much a year for the privilege. Bishop Bronescombe's first appropriations were of Budock to which was united the small church of St Thomas of Penryn, St Gluvias, and Feock. The bishop ordered a perpetual vicar to be appointed in each of the three churches, collation of whom was reserved to himself. Confirmation of the gift of Feock church by Walter Peverell was made on 10th October 1267. Peverell was a founding canon of the college and had already granted it to Budock church. The same day the church of Sithney was appropriated to Glasney after the death or retirement of the then rector. This took place in 1270 and on 21st August of that year Alan de Hellestone was collated as its first vicar. On 1st September 1270 the churches of Sithney, Zennor, St Goran, St Enoder and Kea (with chapels at Kenwyn and Tregavethan) were officially appropriated for the daily distribution amongst the clergy of the college. The bishop at the same time granted thirteen acres of land in Glasney for houses and other buildings for the canons and reservation was made for the stipend of a perpetual vicar in each of the parishes. These churches had come to the bishop from a variety of sources. Roger de Skyburiow had granted him land and the advowson of Sithney and in 1265 Jocinus de Antrenon provided him with land and rights in the same church. In 1269 Philip de Bodrugan granted him land and the advowson of St Goran and around the same time John de Treiagu granted him St Enoder and Stephen Haym, Kea.

While generally the tithes that provided funds for Glasney were the same for each parish, there was some variation. Essentially the great tithes, those on corn, hay, etc. went to the rector and the small tithes, the altalage, those capable of being laid at the altar, went to the vicar. With each appropriation, a taxation of each vicarage was made to clarify exactly what the rectorial institution and the vicar should have. At Budock and the annexed church of Penryn, the altalage was granted to the vicar except for the tithes of fish, wool, lambs, and peas and vetches growing in the fields. The vicar was to have the manse in which the rector of Penryn had been accustomed to dwell and the sanctuary and gardens of Bohellan, St Gluvias. This was in 1270 but the arrangement does not seem to have been satisfactory and following a visitation of Bishop Stapeldon in 1315 he found that the vicar's stipend was insufficient to sustain the ordinary burdens of his benefice. The former taxation was therefore cancelled and, in the new, to the vicar's perquisites were added the tithes of hay growing in meadows in the parishes, already existing or to be made thereafter. The tithes of flax and hemp together with the crops grown in courtlages and cultivated with spades, then and henceforward, and as before, the sheaf tithe, and that of beans, peas, vetches growing in the fields, of wool and lambs were to go to the provost and chapter who were to pay to the vicar 40s. yearly towards the cost of repairing books and remedying other defects in the churches and also to bear any extraordinary burdens of the vicar in the parishes.

At Feock the same initial arrangement was made, except that the vicar had the tithe of fish and the sheaf tithe of the vill, or hamlet, of Tregew and the college was to pay the vicar 'a mark of silver in aid'. At Sithney in 1270, the vicar was assigned the small tithes, the tithes of hay at Ventonvedna and St Elvan and the tithes of peas and beans growing in gardens. He was also granted a dwelling house and gardens and a couple of fields beside the road from Helston to Hayle, while in return he was to discharge all the duties of the place and pay 40s. yearly to the canons of Glasney. At Zennor in 1270 the tithes of fish, wool, beans and peas growing in open fields were reserved to the college while the vicar was granted the manse previously occupied by the rector and the whole of the sanctuary or glebe. As at Budock and Feock, it soon appeared that the vicar was not receiving sufficient revenue and in 1315 Bishop Stapledon ordered that in addition he should have the sheaf tithes (the tithes of hay from meadows already enclosed or to be enclosed) of the vills of Treveglos and Bos, the tithes of flax, hemp, fish, and of crops cultivated by the spade in gardens, then and in the future. The college was no longer to pay him a pension of 20s. yearly but was to make one initial payment of that amount towards the cost of repairing books and remedying other defects, and to bear extraordinary burdens.

The arrangement at St Enoder, made in 1271, was that the vicar was to have the house formerly occupied by the rector, Walter de Fermesham, thirteen acres of glebe land and all the small tithes except those of peas and beans growing in the fields. At Kea in 1270 the vicar was assigned the whole altalage of the mother church and the chapels of Kenwyn and Tregavethan, except the tithes of peas and beans growing in the fields. He was to have the houses and glebe lands attached to the church and chapels and pay a yearly rent to the canons of Glasney of £3. Originally at St Goran in 1270 the vicar had the whole altalage (small tithes, including those of the fishery, apples, beans and peas growing in gardens) the tithes of corn and hay only being excepted. The following year, however, an alteration was made because it was thought to be too favourable to the vicar. Excluded from the vicar's portion were tithes from boats in excess of twelve and the rector's seines; an interesting exclusion showing that seining operations were being conducted there and that investment in seines was being taken up by people who were not fishermen themselves. In compensation though, the vicar was to have one third of the tithe of hay and the college two-thirds only.

While the provost and chapter held ultimate sway regarding the running of temporal matters, it is clear that for this purpose they used lay persons. In the statutes promulgated by Bishop Bronescombe reference was made to stewards and to their treasury and in 1273 it was specifically stated that rents were to be paid quarterly to the steward of the chapter, or his deputy. The college was said to have a treasury in 1445 and the bishop found among other misdeeds that the stewards were in the habit of mixing the money of the college with their private money, and misusing it. In 1536 the college had a steward, Stephen Gayre, and an auditor, John Killigrew, who received respectively 10s. and 20s. annually. The principal task of the steward was the collection of the revenue from the rectories and the few non-ecclesiastical sources of income and the disbursement of stipends and wages to the canons and other residents and employees of the college, the settlement of bills for repairs, maintenance work, new items needed for the church, and the periodic taxes.

The tithes of the rectories were in fact regularly farmed and the canons themselves were accustomed to take the farms, no doubt making some profit that would help boost their income. In the statutes promulgated by Bishop Bronsecombe rules were established for the management of farms. No canon was to receive more than one farm from the chapter and other farms were to be granted to the canons who had no farm, to those who offered most and had made due residence. Farmers who failed to pay their whole rent punctually into the exchequer, by the hands of the steward, were liable to be deprived of their farms — this punishment though was to be at the bishop's discretion. Moreover, establishing the democratic spirit of the college regarding this matter, it was ordered that the more weighty business of the college, such as letting of farms, presenting to benefices etc. was to be transacted by the canons in chapter.

The cartulary provides more details about how the farms were managed. Farmers of the rectories had to pay the assessed rents within the parish of their farms, in equal payments at the four usual terms, Christmas, Easter, the Nativity of St John the Baptist and Michaelmas, although their tenants were not likewise bound to pay their rents at those terms — clearly canons were accustomed to sublet their farms. The rents of the farms were fixed, the competitive element among farmers being apparently the amount of the fine or premium on taking up a lease. The farmer of the corn tithes of St Budock and the tithe of lambs, wool, and fish of the same parish and St Gluvias with the rent of St Budock glebe and Tregoneggy paid £20.7s.5d. in four equal instalments. The farmer of Sithney paid £17 yearly for garb or sheaf tithe, the sanctuary of glebe and the vicar's pension; Zennor paid £12, St Enoder £25 for the garb and sanctuary, Kea £26 for the garb of that church and the chapels of Kenwyn and Tregavethan, the tithe of wool there and the rent of the vicarage; Feock £9.8s.2d. for the garb and for rent, and St Gluvias £10.7s.4d. for the garb with miscellaneous rents.

On account of abuses connected with the letting of farms it was decreed that a farm should not be entrusted to one canon, unless any should voluntarily renounce his farm, in which case its income was to be divided amongst the canons. A document of 1273 provided that whoever received a farm from the chapter should, if he wished, retain it for life, as long as he paid his rent. Terms were to commence on the day after Michaelmas day, and all rents were to be paid quarterly to the steward or his deputy. If the farmer did not satisfy the chapter at any quarter day, he immediately forfeited his farm, with all its appurtenances and all improvements which he might have made and the provost and chapter could dispose of the same as they willed. These arrangements were confirmed at a meeting of the provost and canons on 17th April of that year.

The taxation of Manaccan appropriated to the college in 1275 is not detailed but no doubt the rectorial tithes were the same as customary. The same is the case with Colan, appropriated in 1276. At St Allen, appropriated in 1287 by Bishop Quivil, the vicar had the tithe of stacked corn and hay of Tretherras, the tithe of all produce of the park of Lanner, including the garb, or great tithes, with the whole of the small tithes and glebe, except a grange for a mowhay or rickyard and other purposes which with the right of way to the same were to be retained by the college as rectors of the church; the latter, of course, retained the rectorial tithe, the garb, etc. in this taxation which was drawn up by Bishop Stapeldon in 1314. Mylor was appropriated in 1288. By the taxation of 1353 the vicar held a messuage by the church, the entire altalage of both Mylor and its chapel of Mabe, the tithe of hay and the fishery, mortuaries of the whole parish and the garb tithes of Creggoes, the college retaining the garb tithes of the remainder.

A tax on ecclesiastical properties was initiated by Pope Nicholas IV to provide funds for Edward I to go on crusade against the infidel in the Holy Land. Its assessment gives details of the supposedly actual values of the various rectories and vicarages held by the college. In the deanery of Penryn, the rectory of St Budock was assessed at £6 and St Gluvias £2. In Powder, St Feock was valued at £3.6s.8d., its vicarage 13s.4d., Kea £8.6s.8d., its vicarage £1, and St Allen £5.6s.8d.; Mevagissey which was to come to the college in the fourteenth century was worth £2. In Penwith Zennor was assessed at £4, its vicarage £1 and St Just which was acquired subsequently £8; in Pyder, St Enoder £7.6s.8d., its vicarage £1, Colan £4, its vicarage 6s.8d. This valuation is useful as a comparative guide to the values of the respective rectories though it is generally considered to be an under-assessment. It was preserved in the King's Exchequer and was the basis by which subsequent assessments on the clergy were made until the reign of Henry VIII.

Problems that could arise regarding the farming of rectories are illustrated by what happened at St Goran in the early fourteenth century. William de Bodrugan, a canon and then the Archdeacon of Cornwall, farmed the great tithes of the parish — of corn and hay — in 1300 for £13.6s.8d. yearly. On his death in late 1307 the tithes were said to be worth £40 yearly, so clearly he had not done too badly in the transaction. The farm had been a life grant but when he died his executors claimed the coming autumn crops. Asked for his judgement in the matter, Bishop Stapeldon wrote to the provost and chapter on 20th June of that year expressing the strong opinion that William de Bodrugan's lease had expired with his life. Referring to the customs of the church of Exeter he found that where a canon died before the 20th December, the fruits of the coming autumn belonged not to his estate but to the next farmer, whether he had or had not paid anything towards the cost of the coming year's rent. If, however, he died after that day and had paid any part of the rent, the fruits did then belong to his estate. If he had not paid anything then his estate was only entitled to the amount he had expended in cultivation of the glebe.

A fresh ordinance was made regarding St Goran in 1316 when the provost and chapter, noting that the tithe value of the farm in fact was then £40, assigned the rectorial tithe to necessary expenses of the church of Glasney, including the covering of the roof with lead, while sums accruing above the rent of £13.6s.8d. were to go to resident canons, other church expenses, hospitality towards tenants, and other works of charity. Also it was provided — as if this were a problem previously at St Goran — that farmers should not destroy or allow to be destroyed the woods, parks, gardens, buildings, or other things pertaining to the farms. If any damage were done, the same should be repaired and renewed at the expense of the farmer, before the following Michaelmas, or else a penalty would ensue. Sanctuary land was not to be let to laymen, lest they be subject to distress and lay control. If any laymen were placed within the sanctuary (land belonging to the church where criminals sought refuge in order to get a lesser sentence than they would in common law) by the tithe farmers they should be removed before the following Michaelmas, under pain of canonical penalties and deprivation of their farms.

The harshness of the system is demonstrated by the case of Sir Adam de Carleton, a canon of Glasney, who seems to have succeeded William de Bodrugan to both the archdeaconry of Cornwall and the St Goran farm, in 1308. The archdeaconry was in the gift of the young King Edward II. De Carleton was his chaplain and must have been comparatively young himself since he was to hold the archdeaconry for the next thirty-eight years. At about this time the King's favourite, Piers Gaveston, a Gascon whose arrogance alienated the old nobility, had been made Earl of Cornwall and it seems probable that Sir Adam was one of his circle, Norman-French speaking and out of sympathy with the

Cornish populace. In 1321, when the political temperature was rising with the Earl of Lancaster's rebellion developing in the north and in the south west his supporter, Otto de Bodrugan rallying the opposition, de Carleton's unpopularity was made apparent. For some reason he got into arrears with his farm rent, and although it was only fifteen days overdue, the farm was immediately forfeit and the provost and chapter fixed on a successor, a senior resident canon, Master Richard de Beaupre, who had no farm and who offered better terms than his predecessor. Investigating the matter, the bishop found that Beaupre was entitled to the farm but he considered the provost and chapter were neglectful in doing justice and were also defiant. He ordered them to call the parties together and informed them that further neglect of duty would be subject to penalties. Clearly Sir Adam had rubbed the locals up the wrong way and continued to do so. In 1328 there was a perhaps mischievous report that he was dead and the new King Edward III appointed another to his prebend at Glasney. However Bishop Grandisson, finding that de Carleton was still alive, rejected the new appointment. Unfortunately Sir Adam's unpopularity did not end there. In 1332 he was charged with oppression in his office, and in 1346 he pleaded for an exchange with the archdeaconry of Brington in Huntingdon on the grounds that 'the people amongst whom he found himself were given to fault-finding, undisciplined and difficult to inform or correct. . .moreover at Brington he would be not far from friends and would find his speech better known', adding that 'owing to his inability to personally make the rounds of his archdeaconry he lost practically the whole fruits of his office and the greatest part of his means of living'.

In 1329 two canons, Master Reginald de Campo Arnulphi and Master Benedict de Arundell, were in dispute respecting a farm at Glasney. The provost and chapter proposed to end the dispute by forcing Campo Arnulphi (Champernowne) to accept the farm of the then-vacant church of St Budock or be precluded from the enjoyment of any other that might in future become vacant. The bishop, however, ordered that an interim custodian should be assigned to St Budock and the two disputants were to be heard before his own court. The farms clearly caused friction between canons and their judicious allocation must have been a continuous problem. Tithe-collection which the farms entailed, too, involved sordid commercial activity which cannot have been beneficial to the spiritual life the college was supposed to be encouraging. One way out was by the sub-letting of farms and this certainly did occur, *vide* the case of Master John de Stoke who, on 22nd December 1336, received episcopal licence to sublet his farm to some suitable person.

In the fourteenth century two additional appropriations were made. In 1329 Lamorek or Mevagissey was appropriated — its income was said to amount to £17.1s.4d. By the taxation of that year the provost and chapter were to have the glebe and the great tithes of Treflunen, Higher and Lower Tregassick, Higher Pentewan, Tregiskey Wollas, North Pentewan, Tregiskey Wartha, and Trewinney, the sum of whose great tithes amounted to £8.13s.4d. and all other profits that might accrue from such great tithes. The vicar was to receive a stipend of 5s. from the provost and chapter, the great tithes of the garb of Penwarne, Treleaven, and the vill of Lamorek (i.e. from the south of the parish) and the whole of the altalage and small tithes, oblations, mortuaries, and other obventions from the whole parish. At St Just, which was appropriated in 1355, a taxation of about 1380 assigned to the vicarage all the altalage, including the tithe of hay throughout the parish, of flax, hemp, fish, and all other small tithes. The vicars were to have all the buildings belonging to the church, the rectory-house and the farm and other buildings belonging to the church with the yards and dovecote nearby, but reserving a right to the provost and chapter to use the said buildings when any of them should require to stay there on the business of the church. They were to have seven acres of land in three crofts near the rectory-house, with an additional three acres for the support of their own households. The college was to have the garb. In 1410 the provost and chapter complained to the bishop of the interference of the parishioners of St Just with the collection of the college revenues. Excommunication of the offenders was ordered to be published accordingly.

As well as the church and ancillary buildings, the college did possess some temporalities, i.e. land and non-ecclesiastical sources of income, though minute in comparison to the rectories. In 1536 it was said that the 'yearly value of rents and farms of lands and tenements of both free tenants and conventionaries, with two shillings from the perquisites of the court, were estimated by the commissioners at £4'. This contrasted with £206.13s.2d., the yearly value of garb tithes, etc. In 1291 the temporalities of the college were said to consist of the manor of Penryn worth £21.8s.1¼d. Whether this was an error since the bishopric held the local manor or whether this sum represented what the college then held in rights and lands in the town, is not known. Certainly if the latter is the case their value was dissipated in succeeding years. At the dissolution it was said the college possessed five and a half acres of wood which Thurstan Peter postulated may have referred to the adjacent Bishop's Wood, though this probably formed part of the episcopal estates rather than those of the college.

The lands which the college acquired appears to have been those granted by donors over many years, small parcels from the proceeds of which obits in memory of individuals were paid. Thus in 1315 William de Mulleborne granted the college 'a quarter of an acre of land in Penryn lying between the tenement formerly of Jordan Lowys of that town on the north, the tenement of the portioners of the church of Mynstre [Manaccan] on the south, the land of Master Walter de Bodmin, canon of Glasney on the west, and St Thomas' Street on the east'. In 1321 Benedict Arundell granted the college a messuage and land at Polventen; this was no doubt the tenement which the provost and chapter alienated to Stephen de Reswalstes for his life in 1340: 'a messuage and all their lands of Polventen, enclosed and unenclosed'. Stephen de Hal and Margeria his wife granted the college a messuage in Penryn in 1336; other obits were secured by William, son of Roger de Bodwey, and John and Constance Rous in 1349 and 1356 respectively on a messuage and rents in Penryn. Constance Rous made doubly sure by another grant, of 1377, of tenements in Penryn situated between the church of St Mary, Penryn and the tenement of Richard Beauchamp. Odo Brasigonha granted a messuage in the town in 1369 and in 1380 Walter Myn and John Trevyda three messuages there.

The lands were obviously of no great extent and unlike many other institutions Glasney, being a comparatively late foundation, was unusually dependent on ecclesiastical sources for its revenue. This fact linked the college closely with the tithe-collection system, not a popular facet of life in the Middle Ages. Where the tithes of produce went directly to religious institutions, this caused less resentment than when the collection was in the hands of farmers who were seen to be making considerable profits from the undertaking. The provost was generally identified in this way with tithe-collection, and when he came to take up as a side enterprise tax-collection on behalf of an unpopular monarch, as did Sir John Oby in 1497, it was asking for trouble. His hard dealing in the hundred of Kerrier sparked off a major revolt and he himself was subsequently brutally murdered.

There is little detail available about the garnering of the rectorial tithe in the fifteenth and early sixteenth centuries but absence of material may suggest that the system had become well-established, a routine of the life of the parishes which were affected. When Henry VIII ordered the valuation of 1536, Glasney's rectories were marked up considerably from the time of Pope Nicholas IV. The garb tithes of St Just with the glebe were valued at £21.7s.8d., Zennor £8.12s.2d., Sithney with glebe £20, Budock with glebe £17.8s., St Gluvias £10.10s., Feock £7.13s.4d., Kea and Kenwyn £24.3s.4d., St Goran with glebe £22, St Enoder with glebe £27.13s.4d., Mevagissey £3.6s.8d., Mylor £20, Colan £5.6s.8d., Manaccan £7, St Allen £10.12s. In addition the tithes of Tregonhay in Budock were valued at 15s. and those of Penryn 5s. The increased value between the two periods was no doubt real enough but it is probable that both were undervaluations, especially the first which was an ecclesiastical assessment. It is instructive to compare what farmers paid to have the garb tithes. Thus at the beginning the sum payable by those who took Zennor was £12 compared with the 1291 assessment of £4 and the 1536 one of £8.12s.1d. The rate for Sithney was £17 while in 1536 the valuation was only a few pounds above £20. The farmer of Budock first paid £20.6s.8d., the assessment in 1291 being £6 and in 1536 £17.8s. For St Gluvias £10.7s.4d. was paid in 1291, then £2 and in 1536

£10.10s; for Feock he paid £9.8s.2d., in 1291 £3.6s.8d., and in 1536 £7.13s.4d.; for Kea he paid £26.2s., in 1291 £8.6s.8d., and in 1536 £24.3s.4d.; for St Enoder £27, in 1291 £7.6s.8d., and in 1536 £27.13s.4d.

Sometimes other evidence sheds light on the subject. When St Just was appropriated to Glasney in 1355 a sum of £21.13s. was assigned out of the rectory for the stipends of priests, choristers, etc. This compared with a valuation of £8 in 1291 and £21.7s.8d. in 1536. It is clear that as a source of funds tithes were an inefficient form of accumulation and that much of the profits went to the actual farmers. Moreover some of the opprobrium that their collection naturally attracted inevitably passed on to the college itself, the overt destination for contributions.

In terms of dissolution, Glasney was a simple nut to crack being so dependent on this ecclesiastical source of income, unlike some institutions that also held large estates. This characteristic was no doubt due to the fact that it was a comparatively late creation, a creation above all of an ecclesiastical institution itself, the bishopric of Exeter. Thus, when the time came, the rectories were simply transferred to others (at a price), the buildings sold off lock, stock and barrel and the residents provided with pensions, which, since they should be without dependents and many of whom were aged, would simply conclude with their deaths.

Johanna Kelly, mother of John Kelly,
Canon of Glasney 1431–1448. Tintagel, c. 1430.

CHAPTER VI

Glasney College In The Community

WHILE his dream may have been inspirational, the selection of the site for Glasney undoubtedly owed much to the fact that Bishop Bronesombe had an important power-base in the area already. His landholding was based on the manor of Treliever which had been held by the bishop in 1086 and was probably originally attached to one or more Celtic monasteries in the area. The manor was a sizeable one at Domesday, in all probably about 2,400 acres, and was said to have land for twenty ploughs. The demesne had two ploughs and the villagers twelve, the rest of the acreage presumably being waste. On the demesne were 30 sheep, 2 cows, 5 wild mares, and 16 oxen to operate the two ploughs. When the town of Penryn developed in the twelfth and thirteenth centuries, the manor was divided into Penryn Town and Penryn Foreign, the latter including about half of St Gluvias, Mylor (apart from the manor of Restronguet), the whole of Mabe, Budock, Mawnan, Budock Vean in Constantine, Manaccan (apart from Rosewick), and the fief of Mudgeon in St Martins. The whole area was a bishop's peculiar in which courts were held and wills proved and where other ecclesiastical rights existed outside the jurisdiction of the Archdeacon of Cornwall and answerable directly to the bishop. The manor house and its demesne lay on the south side of Glasney, divided from it by the highroad.

It was in January 1265 that Bishop Bronescombe first began the process of endowing his new college with neighbouring advowsons. On the 12th of that month Master Gervasius de Cridetone resigned his rights in Budock church and on 15th March Master Robert de Peintone resigned his. To Budock he united the small church, apparently the manor chapel, of St Thomas of Penryn. There is a tradition that after the foundation of Glasney the bishop allowed the borough of Penryn a 'moidore' yearly for the loss of the ground from the town. Walter Peverel, one of the founders, granted the college the fruits of Budock and St Feock and by Bishop Bronescombe's charter of 26th March 1267 a perpetual vicar was to be appointed to each of the three churches of St Gluvias, Budock, and Feock; the vicarages of the two former churches were in fact united at an early date (certainly before 1310).

The taxation of the vicarage of St Budock and the church of Penryn annexed to it was made on 21st August 1270. The vicar was then to have the manse in which the rectors of the church of Penryn had been accustomed to dwell, which was obviously within the town. In 1288 the neighbouring church of Mylor was appropriated to the use of the provost of Glasney in perpetuity and a vicar assigned to undertake the religious and pastoral offices necessary in the parish. So by this time a whole block of parishes in and around the college had become linked to it, with their rectors serving as canons and garb tithes and other dues being received by it, all within the sound of its church bells.

Sir Stephen Heym, steward of the Earl of Cornwall and holder of several benefices already in Cornwall, was a founding canon of the college. He built his residence on the east side of the public road going from Penryn to Budock in the wood and separate from those of the other canons. Bronescombe disapproved of this and on the canon's death, probably around 1275, took the place himself. In view of its more than ordinary embellishment and construction he appears to have made it the manor house and bishop's palace, where bishops stayed when on visitations or when for some other purpose were in the area. Sir Stephen was succeeded by a relative, Master Adam Heym, clerk of the earl and likewise holder of several benefices. In compensation for the loss of his residence, the bishop granted him a piece of ground on the north side of the church beyond the river, which had no buildings on it. Adam Heym, however, spent much of his time travelling as a preacher, and neglected to erect the necessary buildings. When his prebend became vacant Bishop Bytton granted it with the site to Master Walter de Bodmin, who completed the residence.

On 13th April 1275 Bishop Bronescombe confirmed the charter of privileges granted to the burgesses of Penryn by his predecessor Bishop Brewer on 29th August 1236. Some idea of the nature of these is revealed in the dispute between the bishop and the earl which was resolved this year. The earl undertook 'to re-erect the pillory and tumbrel of the free borough of Penryn which had been thrown down'; evidence of the roughhouse tactics that had been used in the dispute. In the *Quo Warranto* proceedings at the eyre of 1301 Bishop Bytton claimed for his free borough of Penryn the assise of bread and ale as well as the use of the tumbrell and pillory. The borough jury (twelve in number, which indicates that it was no mini-borough but a reasonably sized town by this period) claimed that it was a borough of the Bishop of Exeter pertaining to the barony of the bishop. As well as the assise of bread and ale, a market was held every Monday and an annual fair on the vigil, day, and morrow of the translation of St Thomas the Martyr, on the 6th, 7th, and 8th July. The privileges were subsequently confirmed by the king.

The jury at the eyre consisted mostly of men with Cornish names, unlike Bodmin and Lostwithiel, which were the principal towns at this time and which had a large foreign element. Chief bailiff was John Trenewith and others were Hugo de Kerigou, John Tregorrek, Walter de Carnduior, Lucas Langeman, Jordan Joy, Shonos Japhes, Richard le Tayler, Galfridus Bastard, Philip de Trewython, Nicholas le Tayler, Richard de Beedlan, and John de Nanfran. Subsequent to the last eyre of 1284 three murders in the town were reported in which two guilty parties were clergy, Bartholomew Hervi and Amandus de Anter, both of whom were handed over to the bishop for punishment. Two robbers were reported as having been hanged. Bartholomew Hervi was also in charge of a wine-selling establishment and according to the contemporary report he was one of two men in the town who had sold two doles of wine contrary to the assise, the other being Andrew Margh. The town must have experienced a considerable wreck in its vicinity sometime before because the value of 'wreck of the sea' since the last eyre was stated to be £13.6s.8d.

The jury of the hundred found in other cases that

the bishop of Exeter holds the manor of Penren of the king in chief worth £30 in which are the advowson of the churches of St Melor, which is worth with the chapel of St Laud per annum £20. And St Budoc which is worth per year 20 marks and St Gywias £10, Munstre [Manaccan] £10, to which King Henry III used to present [in the time of vacations up to 38 years before] which said Walter, formerly Bishop of Exeter appropriated to the church of St Thomas of Glasney and the advowsons of the said churches and appointed secular canons there. After this the bishop comes and says his predecessors acquired the advowsons from divers persons who held nothing in chief of the king.

The rent roll of the bishopric in 1307-8 showed him receiving annually from the borough of Penryn the net sum of £7.1s.3½d., from the market £23.17s.11d. (again a sizeable sum indicating the importance of the town and its market at this time), from aids from soc-men (ordinary tenants) 1s.3d., in lieu of ploughing 3s.6d., in lieu of help in reaping the autumn harvest 2s.0¾d, from rent of land £2.9s.10d., from the farm of four corn mills and one tucking mill £13.6s.8d., for 'berbiage' (probably from *bergeria* meaning sheep-fold) 22 ewes, beside the tithe and acquittance. Pope Nicholas's Taxation of 1292 which gave among the temporalities of the college the manor of Penryn, valued at £21.8s.1¾d., was clearly in error and it belonged then as before to the bishopric. According to the inventory put together on the death of Bishop Bytton, the manorial demesne, on the south side of the college, then carried 5 horses, 39 cattle (made up of 20 oxen, 1 bull, 14 cows, 1 yearling and 3 calves), 155 ewes, 81 wethers, 41 lambs, 3 rams, 4 pigs and 26 goats. This considerable increase from the time of Domesday was a sign of the agricultural improvements in the previous two centuries but no doubt also the demesne had grown in size from what it had been in 1086, when it had been calculated at 240 acres. In 1327 following Bishop Stapeldon's death the numbers of stock had not greatly changed. There were 7 horses, 28 cattle (including 16 oxen, 1 bull, 7 cows and 4 calves), 105 ewes, 146 wethers, 11 lambs, and 2 rams. There were then no pigs or goats and the reduction in the number of cows is explained by the transference of some to the bishop's manor of Lawhitton.

The wood or park on the south side of the college, claimed as a free warren in 1301, caused some problems through poaching, as elsewhere on the bishop's lands in Cornwall. In June 1311 a commission of 'oyer and terminer' was issued touching the persons who had broken into and hunted in the parks of Pawton and Lanner, and in this bishop's free warrens at Pawton, Cargoll, Penryn, Tregear, St Germans, and Lawhitton and had assaulted his men and servants at various places in Cornwall. It must have been Bishop Stapeldon who made the wood into a deer park in subsequent years. But there was still trouble from poachers, and on 5th May 1329 a canon, Sir Ralph Arundell, was absolved from the sentence of excommunication in which he had involved himself by trespassing on the park of Penryn and carrying away some of the goods of the church, presumably deer.

In 1330 Bishop Grandisson wrote to his bailiff at Penryn, saying that he believed the malefactors who had broken into his park there had entered in by way of the enclosure of one of the canons and had made easier entry because of some of the canons' private doors leading from their enclosures into the park, which might be a source of mischief in the future. He asked the bailiff to order the canons and their vicars or proctors to repair the fences of their gardens and lock their doors and to report defaulters for punishment. In February that year a mandate was issued against trespassers of the park, those who 'with devilish daring entered the park and publicly and openly and with mighty clamour, with a view to hunting, and did slay, take and carry away our fallow deer and other wild animals kept therein; and did cut down and burn trees and shrubs growing therein'. He ordered the provost to find out who the offenders were and to excommunicate them. A part of the wall that separated the canons' ground from the West Wood survived to Thurstan Peter's time.

The taxation of St Budock church in 1270 did not prove satisfactory and a fresh deed was made in 1315, in which Bishop Stapeldon noted that during his visitation of the archdeaconry of Cornwall and his peculiars therein, he found that differences had arisen between the provost and chapter of Glasney and Sir Robert, the perpetual vicar of these united benefices, regarding the vicar's portion and other matters. He heard both parties in the chapterhouse of Glasney and made the settlement detailed in the last chapter. On 12th May 1318 the bishop confirmed the grant of the churches of St Budock and St Gluvias to Glasney.

St Thomas's church which Thurstan Peter believes to have been the manor church, was on the site of the present town hall but the borough also had a Chapel of the Blessed Mary which must have been sited a little further down the main highway towards the estuary. The old name for Broad Street was Our Lady's Street, which suggests it was in this vicinity. In 1377 Constance, widow of John Rous, established an obit at Glasney by granting four shillings rent out of a tenement in Penryn, situated between the church of St Mary, Penryn and the tenement of Richard Beauchamp. It was during the provostship of Master Benedict de Arundell, collated in 1313, that there was a dispute between Sir Stephen de Reswalstis, vicar of St Gluvias, and the burgesses of Penryn regarding the portion of the oblations received in the chantry of the Chapel of the Virgin Mary due to the vicar and also the claim of the vicar to the best upper garment of the dead.

A tribunal set up at Glasney to decide on the matter was constituted as a Bishop's Court and presided over by the official of the peculiar jurisdiction of the bishop. The court met on Friday, 8th October 1322 with the burgesses (whose leading members were Laurence Bastarde, Bartholomew Seneschelle, Ralph de Leo, John Urban, and Amideus Taylor) represented by a vicar of Glasney who was the syndic or proctor of the commonalty of Penryn town Sir Andrew Penryn, and the vicar of St Gluvias Sir Stephen de Reswalstis representing himself. The decision of the tribunal was that the chaplain celebrating in the chapel was to receive yearly a stipend of 24s. from the goods of the chapel, and that he was to be presented by the burgesses. All legacies and offerings of candles and ready money at the chapel were to be received by the burgesses, except the Easter offerings made by strangers who were taking communion at that church or at funeral services when the body of the person commemorated there was to be buried in the mother church. For this right the burgesses were to pay to the vicar at the great altar of St Gluvias 12d. on the day of St Gluvias each year 'in a token of subjection duly made to the said mother church'. If they failed to pay this sum, the vicar was entitled, without need of legal process, to suspend the chantry and to obtain its full income. Moreover, the vicar was to have the best upper garment of everyone who was serving or lodging in the borough at his decease 'as of ancient custom due to him', saving all burgesses, taxpayers, cottagers, their wives, sons, and daughters, who were exempt. Parties to the agreement were to observe the terms of the peace made between them for ever.

The agreement is of considerable interest in showing the balance of powers that existed between a town chapel and a mother church at this time. Burials were made at St Gluvias parish church but clearly St Mary's retained quite a degree of independence and was well supported by towns people, being sustained 'at their expenses and upon offerings made in the chapel and upon legacies left'. In 1476, for instance, Thomas Enys near Penryn left 2d. to Mary the Virgin in the chapel of Penryn Borough as well as making bequests to Glasney, the chapel of St Mary Magdalen in Cosawes, and the high altar of St Gluvias 'for my tithes and obligations withheld and forgotten'. John Enys in 1510 left 12d. to the chapel and 12d. for the plate there and also left sums to the image of St Thomas at Glasney and the chapel of Cosawes. St Mary's was probably the chapel for which Bishop Brantyngham gave a licence 'to the inhabitants of the vill of Penryn' in 1374. In 1384 Sir Walter Myn, while perpetual vicar of St Gluvias, was licensed to celebrate divine service in the chapel of the Blessed Mary of Penryn.

The relationship between the town of Penryn and the college can probably be best described as mutually supportive. Certainly there is no evidence of any antagonism between the two. Both were ultimately under the control of the Bishop of Exeter and this fact no doubt united rather than divided. The college's battlements and towers fronting the creek gave protection to both the residents and the town and it is said that ordnance for the towers was provided and manned by the townspeople. Behind these defences both were able to prosper. There is no evidence of serious trouble being caused through the payment of tithes in the parishes around, as there was at St Just in the early fifteenth century. One expects that tithes were more acceptable if people saw that they were going ultimately to the support of an institution in their midst which was of value and benefit to the community. Work was provided by the establishment for the usual trades of masons, carpenters, smiths, purveyors of food and drink, tailors, cobblers, saddlers, and the whole range of occupations needed to sustain an ecclesiastical institution of this kind. Moreover, exotic educated tastes no doubt stimulated the trade of the port from an early date.

As with the case of Andrew de Penryn, the vicar who represented the town in the 1322 settlement, many of the people of the college, especially among the lower ranks were drawn from Penryn and the surrounding area. A founding canon was Sir Roger de Sancto Constantino, clearly from the neighbouring parish, while the provost in the late 1320s was Richard Seneschall who may have been related to the Penryn family of that name. Clearly, though, most of the canons and the upper echelons were drawn from a wider circle; clerics who had made their mark and were noticed by the bishop. This was especially so before 1400. In the later period, it is noticeable that several bore Cornish names such as Rauf, Rowe, Pascoe, Harry, Nans, Nicholls, etc. and it could be that some of these had Penryn connections. Master Benedict Killigrew, instituted in 1478, was obviously of the local family of that name. When it comes to the lesser ranks of vicars, chantry priests, choristers, and servants, the preponderance of locals becomes clear. Few vicars are named but of those who are the majority were of Cornish origin. The already mentioned Andrew de Penryn came from the town and in 1373 there was Ralph Cosawes who obviously came from the adjacent manor of that name. Alexander Peryne was in charge of the de Ponte chantry from 1541 to 1545. When the bishop held an ordination to the first tonsure at Glasney in 1373 the overwhelming majority of the candidates, 64 in number, were of local extraction. Not all these were going on to service at Glasney but no doubt some did. As the college neared its end the local and Cornish connection became stronger. More than half the canons in 1536 appear to have Cornish names and the majority of those pensioned off at the dissolution; the provost, resident canons, vicars, and choristers;

would seem to have been local.

After 1450 the bishops do not seem to have paid much close attention to their Cornish estates and it is believed that the park at Penryn, like those at Lanner and Pawton, was disparked, i.e. returned to normal management, at about this time. This must have lessened the likely cause of tension between the bishop and his tenants and the college at Penryn as it removed a temptation to poaching, until, that is, the time of Sir James Gentle, who was accused of trespassing against his poorer neighbours. It was no doubt good for the relations of the college and its reputation that its last provost, Master John Libbe clearly of local extraction and a man 'well-learned' was a staider sort than Sir James, so that when the college closed good memories may have been left in the minds of the locals.

There is no doubt that at the dissolution regrets at its closure were uppermost among the majority. Though evidence is sparse on this point, the college certainly played an important part in local charity work, assisting the poor and sick. It is known that at major ceremonies donations were made to the poor and at the dissolution it was said the bell ringer was also engaged in teaching. A. L. Rowse noted that the local commissioners in 1547-48, putting their thoughts to Glasney, approached the place with some solemnity and discretion: 'we detect an unmistakable desire on the part of the commissioners to save something of Glasney for their county'. Undoubtedly some local people benefited from its closure, for instance, the Killigrews and others who could lay their hands on the spoils. It was at this time that the market-house was built, probably on the site of the old church of St Thomas; certain jewels of St Gluvias Church to the value of £20 were put towards the work, although probably as a sop for the locals to see that they too were benefiting from the dissolution. It is ironic that as the towers and defence-works of the college were crumbling, profits from the dissolution of the monasteries were used by the Tudor monarchs towards the construction of the castles of St Mawes and Pendennis to defend Falmouth haven. Within these defences, in the following century, grew the new town and port of Falmouth, which by 1700 had surpassed the old medieval port in trade and size of population. Penryn's prosperity was linked to that of its college; with its removal came decline.

CHAPTER VII

Glasney And The Cornish Language

WHEN Bishop Grandisson assumed the bishopric in 1328 he described his diocese to his superior cardinals at Rome: 'the diocese, which takes in Devon and Cornwall, is divided from other parts of England, and for its sole prospect, one excepted, is bounded on all sides by the ocean, rarely however, navigable, which it is the custom for the inhabitants only to use. The language, also, in the extreme parts of Cornwall is known not to the English but to the Bretons'. It is clear from this reference that the area in which Cornish was spoken was already being reduced; English was probably already beginning to take over in eastern parts. A canon of Glasney, Master John Mooreman, who became vicar of Menheniot in 1530 and who was a native of Southill, is reputed to have been the first who taught the inhabitants of his parish the Lord's Prayer, the Creed, and the Ten Commandments in the English tongue. This is sometimes adduced as evidence that Cornish was still spoken in the easterly parish at this time. However, Richard Gendall the Cornish language expert believes this unlikely, considering that Cornish probably declined in the parish in the fourteenth and fifteenth centuries. The language used for religious services was Latin and Dr Moreman, as he later became, no doubt taught his parishioners the religious nostrums in the language that they were currently using amongst themselves for everyday concerns.

It was a different matter, though, in the centre and west of Cornwall. In 1583 in an Exchequer court case at Gorran Haven over the payment of head-fish to the lord of the manor at Bodrugan, an interpreter had to be called in because certain of the fishermen 'could not well speak or understand English'. It is probable that the language in use among the populace in Kerrier and in and around Penryn and the college throughout the period of its existence was Cornish. Master Adam Murymouthe, precentor of Exeter, took a prebend at Glasney in 1314 but exchanged it with Master John de Lancestone in 1318 for one at Exeter cathedral. One reason for sanctioning the change was that Murymouthe did not know Cornish: *'propter Linguam Parcium Cornubie quam non nostis'*. In 1346 Sir Adam de Carletone sought an exchange with a rectory in Huntingdonshire, partly because he would be better understood there. In 1355 the provost of Glasney, Sir Richard de Gomersale, was appointed with others as a penitentiary in the archdeaconry of Cornwall for those who knew both languages. Judging from his name he was not local and previously he had connections with east Devon monastic houses but, after his obtaining a prebend at the college, in 1329, he would seem to have learnt Cornish, as must have been necessary for one settling at this time at Glasney. In 1355, though, for those Cornish who knew no English Roger Tyrel of the Truro Friary was appointed penitentiary in the archdeaconry.

Passion plays grew naturally out of the religious services celebrating Easter, just as Nativity plays developed from the Christmas celebrations. It is clear that plays were staged in the church at Glasney. In 1360 Bishop Grandisson issued a prohibition addressed to the provost and chapter as well as to the authorities at Ottery, Exeter cathedral, and the collegiate church of Crediton regarding the acting of plays in the churches during the Christmas holidays and on certain Saints' days. Under pain of excommunication, such unseemly and improper pastimes were forbidden. The provost and chapter, like the authorities in the other establishments, promised to stop the abuse, but it seems unlikely that dramatic instruction of this kind ceased totally. Scenic effects became more skilled, trade guilds in the towns became involved and this manner of interesting and entertaining the people was used to put over the Christian message. At Glasney the plays would have been produced in the Cornish language. That this dramatic tradition continued over several centuries at Penryn, even after the Reformation, is shown by an incident that occurred in the town in 1567. A company of actors was playing late at night in the town when

certaine Spaniards were landed the same night. . .with intent to take the towne, spoyle and burne it; when suddenly even upon their entrance, the players (ignorant as the towne's men of any such attempt) presenting a battle on the stage, with their drums and trumpets strooke up a lowde alarme: which the enemy hearing, and fearing they were discovered, amazedly retired, made some few idle shots in a bravado, and so in a hurly-burly fled disorderly to their boats. At the report of this tumult, the towne's men were immediately armed, and pursued them to the sea. . .

It was a different type of theatre by then; the passion and nativity plays were too closely associated with the old church but no doubt it drew on the same desire among the people for some entertainment, colour, and drama in their lives.

The plays that have come down to us in the Cornish language are few enough. The most important is a trilogy known as the Ordinalia, comprising *The Creation of the World*, *The Passion of Christ*, *The Resurrection of our Lord*, *Gwyreans an Bys* (The Creation of the World), partly based on and partly independent of the Ordinalia, and a long play dealing with the life and works of St Meriasek, *Bewnans Meriasek*. They are in many respects parallel to the English medieval cycles, such as the town-plays of Chester, Coventry, and Beverley but they have certain marked features of their own. Thus they omit, somewhat strangely, all references to the Nativity. But more importantly a characteristic distinguishing the Cornish plays from the English is that they draw more upon legends for their material. This ties in with a feature of Cornish churches; their pictorial demonstrations of religious scenes in the painted rood-screens, carved bench-ends, and richly painted windows.

It is known that the manuscript of the *Life of St Meriasek* was completed in 1504 by Dominus Hadton who is believed to have been a canon of Glasney. Internal evidence in the Ordinalia confirms that this too had a likely Glasney provenance, for the plays contain a large number of place names chiefly of that area. King David, preparing to build the temple, rewards a messenger with lands at Carnsew and Trehembys, while Solomon, pleased with its progress, rewards workers with the parish of Budock and Carrak Ruan. On the completion of the temple they are given

> Together with all the fields of Bohellan
> And the wood of Penryn wholly,
> All the water-course;
> The island and Arwinnick,
> Tregenver and Kegellick. . .

Moreover, it is to be noted that a large part of the third play, *Resurrectio Domini*, is taken up by the doubting of Thomas and, of course, Glasney itself was dedicated to a St Thomas, though of a different age.

The Ordinalia is believed to have been written in the second half of the fifteenth century, with the *Bewnans Meriasek*, completed as the sixteenth century began. It seems clear that it was this period that saw an efflorescence of Cornish culture at the college when, as has been noted, Cornish influence by way of personnel was also at its greatest. There were no doubt other plays commemorating individual saints, which have not survived but it is interesting that Camborne's patron saint St Meriodec (the Cornish name for Meriasek) should have had such attention paid to him at Glasney. Within the play there are numerous references to places and events in west Cornwall, Penwith, and Kerrier. King Teudar, the pagan Cornish tyrant, with associations in the Hayle area, was a central figure. When the play was written Henry Tudor was on the English throne and, following the 1497 rebellions and the banishing of popular figures like Henry Bodrugan, the new king was *persona non grata* with the Cornish people. When Teudar was routed on the stage in 1504, the 184 'manucaptors' representing nearly every parish in Cornwall, who had all had to pay heavy fines after the rebellion, must have been very well pleased.

The basis of the play, however, is the life of St Meriodec in Brittany. The version in Cornish has added a few episodes known about the saint's life in Cornwall, plus some local colour. The life is the sole surviving example of a class of vernacular drama once very popular in Cornwall, as it was in Brittany: a religious play based on the life of a saint. It shows an intimate knowledge of Breton traditions and liturgical books and it is clear that the Cornish author had before him a copy of the Breton life of the saint, whose memory was cherished in the diocese of Vannes. It is evidence of the links that must have existed between Catholic Cornwall and Catholic Brittany in the fifteenth and early sixteenth centuries. From a complaint of a Truro custom-house officer, Alexander Carvannel, in 1537, it is known that in that year a party of Cornishmen, accompanied by the vicars of Newlyn East and St Agnes, went on a 'pope-holy pilgrimage' to Lantreger (Treguier) and undoubtedly such visits were common before the Reformation. Perhaps on one such pilgrimage a canon of Glasney, either at Treguier or Saint Jean-du-Doigt (a famous pilgrimage chapel situated on the coast and known to have possessed a life of St Meriodec) may have seen and made a copy of the life.

In Cornwall St Meriodec has no dedication outside Camborne and it is interesting to see the links that had grown up between the parish and Glasney in the fifteenth century. Patrons of the living were the Bassetts of Tehidy who were anciently established there and claimed Norman ancestry. That they would have promoted Cornish language activists *per se* seems unlikely, though being in a strong Cornish-speaking area they probably bowed to the inevitable by having as rectors men who could be completely at one with their congregations. Certainly in Richard II's reign men from outside Cornwall such as the Herle, Colshull, and Assheton families, acquired positions and estates in Cornwall, and it could be that the older-established gentry tended to emphasise their local links. The Bassetts veered if at all to the Yorkist camp in the later fifteenth century and it was established Yorkist policy to build up support among the lower ranks of society and also to play on Britain's Arthurian and Celtic inheritance. It could well be, therefore, that the Bassetts gave tacit, if not overt, support to the Cornish cultural efflorescence, centred on Glasney, that occurred at this time.

Master John Pascoe, who was rector of Camborne for forty-four years, seems to have been a guiding light in the resurgence of interest in things Cornish and in the Cornish language and literature. The fifteenth century was a time of growing trade and social activity, and certainly in law and government the English language was making great strides. Though overtly for other reasons, it could well be that the uprisings that took place in Cornwall in 1497 were caused primarily by the objection of Cornish people to having their language and identity subsumed under the English ethos, as was so obviously happening.

Master Pascoe, clearly of a local family, was still quite a young man when he was recommended by the Bassetts to Camborne. He seems to have come from the Helston area and was early attached to the church of St Keverne. He must have shown talent in his youth for on the bishop's nomination he attended Exeter College, Oxford where he subsequently obtained his Master's degree. He was ordained an acolyte at Clyst on 23rd February, 1426 and received his tonsure at Helston on 19th August, 1427. On the nomination of the abbot and convent of Rewley he was ordained subdeacon at Chudleigh on 24th September, 1429, deacon at the same place the following 17th December, and a priest at Crediton on 1st April, 1430. As John Pascowe, clerk, he was given authorization to work outside the diocese and when nominated to Camborne, aged thirty and more, was described as a chaplain; in the interim he must have served in a chapel, presumably away from Cornwall. On 18th February, 1451, along with others, 'Master John Pascowe, rector of Camborne' was appointed a penitencer, that is, was licensed to receive penances and hear confessions. At some stage in these years he was also to obtain the rectory of Lanreath.

It is not known when he first obtained a prebend at Glasney but it must have been before 29th September, 1463, when he is recorded as sacristan of the college. He was instituted to another prebend, that vacated by Master Thomas Abdy, on 14th June, 1467 at Penryn by Master Owin Lloide, Doctor of Laws, the chancellor of the bishop and obviously a Welshman, instead of by the provost, who was then probably Michael Trewinnard. At the same time he gave up the position of sacristan, to which he was succeeded by Master Thomas Kaylleway. He resigned this prebend on 30th November, 1476 on his being collated to the provostship. He must have been nearing seventy, but in the next fifteen years as a profound, well-schooled Cornishman he exerted a patriotic influence over the activities of the college. It was a difficult period politically, with the demise of Edward IV, the brief disruptive reign of Richard III, and the Tudor takeover of Henry VII. Disenchanted with the central regime, with no active Duke of Cornwall to exercise a directing influence over the region, Cornish people must have looked to their own heritage, their own strengths and character. Their culture was preserved in their language and in the old religious plays, which served as entertainment for the people and as a diversion from the unstable times, but which could not be regarded as subversive by a nervous regime. It must have been under the old, venerable provost that productions of the plays were fostered and fortunately and unusually committed to paper.

Master Pascoe's involvement in Camborne, clearly still a largely Cornish speaking parish, accentuated his concern for Cornish drama. It had been the practice of bishops of Exeter since Bronescombe's time to encourage the replacement of church dedications to the old Celtic saints by more common dedications to Latin saints. At Camborne they were trying to replace the old dedication to St Meriodec by that of St Martin. When Bishop Lacy made enquiry regarding the presentation of John Pascoe to the rectory of Camborne, it was to the parish church of St Martin and not Meriasek that he referred. The Bassett family, patrons of the living, proud of their Norman ancestry, may have been equally anxious to invoke St Martin. It was with this background that St Meriasek's play was put together, with the aid of age-old Breton contacts, as a most effective way of promoting the cause of the Celtic saint. Advocates of St Martin may have said that St Meriasek was an insignificant figure about whom almost nothing was known save a bit of idle gossip, and peasant superstition about a well and a rock. Unlike the other Cornish plays the whole drama is the biography of a saint, not a portion of inspired or apocryphal scripture, and it was intended to place St Meriasek on a pedestal as a saint to be venerated, stressing always his devotion to the Virgin Mary, a popular cult figure at both Camborne and Glasney.

The balance of probability is that the author of the play drew upon a group of Camborne traditions about Meriasek, possibly written down, but more probably oral, and linked to such visible features as the saint's chapel, the well, and the rock. Similarities with the life of neighbouring Gwinear are explained if fifteenth century Camborne traditions were influenced by the general run of similar saints' lives, either written or oral, then current in west Cornwall. As a basis, moreover, there was the saint's life recorded in Breton traditions.

The milieu of late fifteenth century Glasney and the sacristanship and provostship of Master John Pascoe, were clearly favourable to the production of Cornish literary works, but other men, no doubt under his influence, carried on the work. At the end of the St Meriasek manuscipt were the words *'Finitur per dominum Hadton anno domini ML VC IIII'* (completed by Sir Hadton in 1504). Gilbert Doble believes Hadton is a misreading for Rad.Ton meaning an individual named Radulph Ton who was probably a priest and vicar of Glasney. The first ten pages of the manuscript are not in the hand of Radulph or Ralph Ton and seem to have been written without the stage-directions needed for a performance. It seems likely therefore that Ralph Ton was simply engaged in making a prompt copy of the drama, which had been compiled some while before.

Master John Pascoe resigned the provostship in the autumn of 1491. He was succeeded by Sir John Oby, who had previously held the sacristanship. Whether or not he was of a local family is not known. He had been instituted to a canonry in 1478 but resigned this the following year when he became sacristan. He was described then as a chaplain. He seems to have been a good administrator and on Master Pascoe's resignation was collated provost. He was also vicar of St Gluvias but, as previously related, came to a sticky end. A collector of Henry VII's unpopular taxes in 1497 in Kerrier, his meticulous interpretation of the assessments provoked local ire and promoted the rebellion that developed from St Keverne parish. Subsequently he was murdered in Somerset. He seems an unlikely character to have played a part in the Cornish literary revival of these years.

Two more significant figures were Master John Nans and Alexander Penhylle. John Nans was a talented man, of Cornish background, who attended the university of Oxford where he became doctor of both laws. He went on to Bologna in 1481 and became rector of both universities there. He then spent a period in Herefordshire, being admitted to a prebend at Putson Minor in that county in about 1489 and in November 1490 was collated to that of Gorwall and Overbury in the cathedral there. The pull of the south-west was present, however, and in the early 1490s he became vicar of Gwennap and acquired a prebend at Glasney. He was obviously seen as a stabilising influence by Bishop Redmayne and it was he who succeeded Sir John Oby as provost in 1497. At the same time he was appointed the bishop's vicar-general in spirituals and it was in that capacity that he instituted his successor at Gwennap, James Trevethan, on his own resignation in 1497. The years succeeding the Cornish rebellions of 1497 were difficult times, with heavy fines being inflicted on those who had taken part, and a brooding resentment among the people, who had risen twice in one year against the Tudor regime. Only four years later John Nans himself resigned and on 5th June, 1501, in a double exchange at the chapter-house in Exeter, his positions of provost and vicar of St Gluvias were taken on by Master Alexander Penhylle while he was instituted to the rectories of St Illogan and St Meriodec of Camborne, vacated by Penhylle. Not long after he was briefly rector of Redruth, being instituted in 1504, but resigning again in April 1505. He held a variety of other positions in the south-west but perhaps ill-health was the explanation for his brief tenures; by the autumn of 1508 he was dead and replacements were being sought for the rectories of Camborne and Illogan.

John Nans seems an unlikely author of the miracle play, *Bewnans Meriasek*, in view of the time he spent away and his many outside interests. However, he was probably a supporter of the Cornish literary revival at Glasney, and perhaps it was due to his insistence that in 1501, when he was instituted to Camborne parish church, it was documented as being dedicated to St Meriodec, not St Martin.

Like Nans, Penhylle was a well educated man; he probably attended Exeter College, Oxford and achieved a bachelorhood of Decrees. He obviously had good credit with the Bassett family, the main power in the area, who held the patronage of Illogan as well as Camborne, for in November 1493 he was appointed to the rectory of the former church. He was instituted to a prebend at Glasney in August 1495 on the resignation of Master Thomas Acchim. As has been seen, it was following Nans's tenure of the provostship and the vicarage of St Gluvias that he was instituted to both in exchange for Illogan and Camborne, having taken the latter himself only the previous year. These were troubled times and like Nans he was probably seen as an educative and calming influence in the area. As an author of the plays, though, he again seems not to be a likely possibility. It is probably to lesser ranks in the college that one should look for the answer, to members of the full-time staff, for instance vicars associated with Radulph Ton, who spent time in the scriptorium and were involved in the life of the local community, particularly in the production of plays. The role of Penhylle, like Nans, was probably as sympathetic head of the college, who provided the right sort of atmosphere in which such plays could be performed and, fortunately, committed to paper.

Whether one should see the evident literary efflorescence at Glasney as part of a wider campaign to preserve the Cornish cultural tradition, a campaign in which old families like the Bassetts sympathised and which was demonstrated by popular resistance in the two rebellions of 1497, cannot be proved. However, there can be little doubt that the surviving jewels of Cornish literature are closely related to the more Cornish-orientated institution that Glasney became in the late fifteenth century and that, for general encouragement much was owed to men such as John Pascoe, John Nans, and Alexander Penhylle, who had in common that they were of native Cornish stock, were talented men who had done well in their university training, and had returned home to serve in the land of their origin and who had the support of an old established and powerful family, the Bassets.

The demise of Glasney College in 1549 was a blow to the pride of the old order in Cornwall and, undoubtedly, in view of the esteem in which it was held in west Cornwall, its closure was a factor in the rising that took place in Cornwall that year. Already in 1548 the activities of an unscrupulous individual, William Body, who had purchased the archdeaconry of Cornwall, had provoked trouble in the west. The whole tenor of the Protestant regime was proving antipathetic to the old Catholic order. Body, in making a visitation of Penwith, had called together a multitude of parishes instead of examining them separately and, further, had given the impression that the church goods were to be confiscated for the use of the crown. In the spring of 1548 Godolphin, at the head of the commission, produced his report regarding the dissolution of the collegiate churches, chantries, and guilds. The big priories of the east Cornish towns had been dissolved in 1536 and now it was the turn of the main surviving large establishment in the west, Glasney College. While the commission was pursuing its work, new proclamations were being made in London. The use of traditional rites, candles on Candlemas day, ashes on Ash Wednesday, palms on Palm Sunday, creeping to the cross, and the making of holy bread and water were forbidden, and in February 1548 the order was made for the complete removal of images from the churches. Stirrings began in St Keverne parish, led by a mass-priest Martin Geoffrey, and William and John Kilter of Constantine, and supported by men from the area. On 5th April, 1548, a large mob attacked the house in Helston where William Body was staying and murdered him.

This outbreak was pacified, though the ring-leaders were taken and executed, Martin Geoffrey at London, William Kilter, Pascoe Trevian, and others at Launceston, and one at Plymouth. The work of the Reformation continued. In January 1549 the Act of Uniformity was passed and the Book of Common Prayer, to which all services were to conform was introduced. The simplicity of the services rendered redundant many of the church ornaments and plate, and further commissions were appointed in every county to make a survey of the goods each church held. The Prayer Book service was ordered to be used throughout the country on Whit Sunday, 9th June. This provoked opposition that led to violence at Sampford Courtenay in Devon, and in Cornwall Humphrey Arundell of Helland and John Winslade of Tregarrick headed another rising. Bodmin was a centre of opposition with its mayor, Henry Bray, to the fore. Encouraged by their priests, men marched thither from all over Cornwall and, setting up camp, their leaders worked on articles of supplication to the king. The later stages of the rebellion are well known; the siege of Exeter, the defeat of the Cornish contingent by Russell and his foreign mercenaries at Fenny Bridges, the relief of Exeter, the battle of Clyst Heath, the crushing of the Cornish force at Sampford Courtenay and the cruel retribution that Russell thereafter took in Cornwall.

While the dissolution of Glasney College was only one of the factors that caused men to rebel in Cornwall, it was an important one in the area where it had influence. The religious changes and the extinction of the college combined to give rise to unrest. The language which the college had come to serve and promote, the native language, was in the minds of those who drew up the articles at Bodmin. Among these were demands to return to the Latin mass, because they understood no English. 'And so we Cornish men (whereof certain of us understand no English) utterly refuse this new English'. The Protector, Somerset, pertinently replied by asking why those who had no English should object since they certainly understood no Latin, and that he was informed there were very few towns in Cornwall 'but ye shall find more in them that understand English than understand Latin'. The articles drew replies subsequently from Archbishop Cranmer and Nicholas Udall. The latter considered that the rebels had been led astray by the priests and made the excellent suggestion that the new form of service should be translated into Cornish and 'so could be enjoyed by them as well as the rest of the country'. Unfortunately the suggestion was never carried into effect, and the Prayer Book became one of the chief instruments in the spread of the English language in Cornwall.

The rebellion drew support from St Keverne and parishes in the vicinity of Glasney even after the outbreak of 1548. When the siege of Exeter began, among their chief supporters was Robert Welsh, a Penryn man who was vicar of St Thomas's, Exe Island, just outside the west gate. It is recorded that he was of an attractive mien, a good sportsman, archer, and, as was natural for a Cornishman, a good wrestler. He had a hand in the counsels of the rebels, was said to have been instrumental in hanging a man from Tavistock, a Protestant spy who was engaged in carrying letters between his master and Lord Russell at Honiton, but also, toward the end of the siege, had used his influence to prevent the firing of the city. This, however, did not save him from a barbarous death. A gallows was erected on the top of his church tower and there he was hanged in chains in his mass-vestments, 'having a holy-water bucket, a sprinkle, a sacring bell, a pair of beads and such other popish trash hanged about him'. He took his death very patiently and with quiet courage, nor did he confess that he had been wrong in fighting for what he believed.

The defeat of the rising signalled the end of overt opposition to the changes. Essentially religious in origin, a nascent Cornish nationalism was also stifled. Glasney College fell into the hands of the vultures; the buildings deteriorated, and were quarried into. As well as being a meritorious religious institution which provided a stabilising, educative influence in central and western Cornwall in the late Middle Ages, the college came to be a safeguard for the cultural heritage and identity of the people. In many ways the end of Glasney was a damaging blow to the history and spirit of the Cornish nation.

Thomas Trembas, Parson. St. Michael Penkivel, 1515.

Sources

G. H. Cook, *English Collegiate Churches*, Phoenix House, 1959

Julian Cornwall, *Revolt of the Peasantry*, Routledge & Kegan Paul, 1977

Gilbert H. Doble, *The Saints of Cornwall*, Part One, Truro, 1960

G. R. Dunstan ed., *The Register of Edmund Lacy*, Devon and Cornwall Record Society, 1963-72, 5 vols.

L. E. Elliott-Binns, *Medieval Cornwall*, Methuen, 1955

A. B. Emden, *Register of Oxford University*, 3 vols, Oxford

F. C. Hingeston-Randulph, *Episcopal Registers of the Diocese of Exeter*, (volumes concerned with the bishops before Lacy and published in the late 19th century)

G. Oliver, *Monasticon Dioceses Exoniensis*, Exeter, 1846

Thurstan Peter, *History of Glasney Collegiate Church*, Camborne, 1903

A. L. Rowse, *Tudor Cornwall*, Cape, 1941

Lawrence S. Snell, *The Suppression of the Religious Foundations of Devon and Cornwall*, Marazion

Rev. C. R. Sowell, 'The Collegiate Church of St Thomas of Glasney', *Journal of the Royal Institution of Cornwall*, Vol.I, 1865

Charles Thomas, *Christian Antiquities of Camborne*, St Austell, 1967

John A. C. Vincent, 'The Glasney Cartulary', *Journal of the Royal Institution of Cornwall*, Vol.VI, 1878-81

Index

119